Praise for *It's Not Who You Know, It's Who Knows You!*

"This book could make a big difference in the way you build your business. David Avrin's ideas will breathe new life into your brand and set you apart from the rest. "Get out there and be noticed! Read this book!"

—**Ken Blanchard, coauthor of** *The One Minute Manager*® **and** *Leading at a Higher Level*

"Sensible, practical advice on the only way to build a brand in today's overcommunicated society. Companies live or die with PR, so get a head start in the game by first reading David Avrin's well-written book."

—**Al Ries, co-author of** *War in the Boardroom,* *The 22 Immutable Laws of Branding,* **and** *Positioning: The Battle for Your Mind*

"David Avrin has written a great guide to the only kind of marketing that works—doing what we say we'll do, delivering on the promise, and truly meeting the needs of others. This is a book full of useful advice, delivered with integrity."

—**Keith Ferrazzi, author of** *Who's Got Your Back* **and** *Never Eat Alone*

"A very enjoyable read! To win in business today, you have to create a competitive advantage. In this terrific and very insightful book, David Avrin reveals some wonderfully creative strategies to help you effectively stand out in a crowded marketplace, create visibility and buzz, and promote your unique brand—you!"

—**Dr. Tony Alessandra, author of** *The Platinum Rule* **and** *Charisma*

"With memorable examples and a playful conversational tone, David Avrin shows, clearly and concisely, how to differentiate yourself, build your brand, and generate news media coverage to grow your business."

—**Rafael Pastor, CEO and Chairman of the Board of Vistage International**

"David Avrin knows about visibility. This book is filled with common sense and effective strategies to be seen, get known, and stand out. Read this book with a pen in hand. Take notes, create a plan, and apply the knowledge—but only if you really want to be successful!"

—**Shep Hyken, author of** *Moments of Magic,* *The Loyal Customer,* **and** *The Cult of the Customer*

"David Avrin's book heads you into the land of differentiation, which happens to be the key to success or failure of companies, products, and even people."

—Jack Trout, author of *In Search of the Obvious,* and co-author of *Differentiate or Die* and *Positioning: The Battle for Your Mind*

"David Avrin's easy-to-read book is full of great ideas and sage advice on creating picture-perfect moments that will raise your company's profile. Every company has the potential to be as memorable as this modern guide to business success!"

—Jeffrey Hayzlett, Chief Marketing Officer, Eastman Kodak Company

"With today's search resources and tools, the marketing question is no longer 'Can anyone find me or my company?' Rather, the key question every executive ought to be asking is 'What's being said once I'm found?' In his breakthrough book, David Avrin teaches us how having the right people say the right things at the right time about you and your firm is the key to twenty-first-century marketing success. Buy it. Read it—often."

—Sam Richter, Senior Vice President/Chief Marketing Officer, ActiFi; award-winning author of *Take the Cold Out of Cold Calling*

"Many of us have missed the point. We seek friends on Facebook and followers on Twitter, without realizing that it's not about how many we can acquire. It is completely about how many choose to be engaged with us. David Avrin's terrific new book is a must-read in today's hyper-competitive, ultra-connected times. Buy it, read it—but, more importantly, apply its lessons!"

—Scott McKain, author of *The Collapse of Distinction: Stand Out and Move Up While Your Competition Fails* and the #1 business best sellers *What Customers REALLY Want* and *ALL Business Is Show Business*

"Your success is ultimately linked to who knows you and how they know you. David Avrin has written a terrific guide for growing your brand and putting more money in your pocket."

—Mark LeBlanc, President, Small Business Success; author of *Growing Your Business!*

"I really like the premise of this book! Dave Avrin has written an engaging and practical guide about how to stand out and over your competition. It will make you think and will inspire you to act."

—Mark Sanborn, best-selling author of *The Fred Factor, You Don't Need a Title to Be a Leader,* and *The Encore Effect*

IT'S NOT WHO
YOU KNOW
IT'S WHO
KNOWS YOU!

IT'S NOT WHO
YOU KNOW
IT'S WHO
KNOWS YOU!

THE SMALL BUSINESS GUIDE TO RAISING YOUR PROFITS BY RAISING YOUR PROFILE

DAVID AVRIN

WILEY

JOHN WILEY & SONS, INC.

Published by John Wiley & Sons, Inc., Hoboken, New Jersey.

Published simultaneously in Canada.

For general information on our other products and services or for technical support, please contact our Customer Care Department within the United States at (800) 762-2974, outside the United States at (317) 572-3993 or fax (317) 572-4002.

Wiley also publishes its books in a variety of electronic formats. Some content that appears in print may not be available in electronic books. For more information about Wiley products, visit our web site at www.wiley.com.

ISBN 978-0-470-48324-4

Printed in the United States of America.

10 9 8 7 6 5 4 3 2 1

For Mom
Everyone, and I mean everyone, knew my Mom

CONTENTS

ix

The Path to Visibility: Part 2 – Creating Awareness

The Path to Visibility: Part 3 – The Pitch

FOREWORD

A few years ago, a young accountant opening his own practice rented the office next to ours. He had spent a few years with a large accounting firm, and was now ready to take the leap and go out on his own. Every day, I'd pass his open door and see him sitting at his desk—all alone. No clients. No ringing phone. It just wasn't happening for this guy.

One day, he timidly entered our offices and asked if he could have a few minutes of my time. He took a deep breath and said "I'm in trouble. I'm just not getting any business. I can't really figure out what's wrong, because I'm good at what I do and I know that I can give people great service. I know you help companies become more competitive. What advice do you have for me? What am I doing wrong?"

I looked him straight in the eye and said, "Nobody knows you exist. That can be a problem."

If only David Avrin's book, *It's Not Who You Know, It's Who Knows You!* had been around back then, I could have just handed the young accountant a copy and said, "Read this and do what it says." It would have changed his world. More to the point, he would have gotten some customers and made some money.

This poor accountant was, admittedly, a very extreme example of a guy without a clue. But the sad fact is that many, if not most businesses and entrepreneurs, suffer from some degree of the same cluelessness. They think that if they are really good at what they do, the world will beat a path to their door. If only that were true.

The fact is that if you're really good at what you do, that gets you even with all of your competitors, who are also really good at what they do. Think they're not good? Oh, grow up. If they weren't good at what they do then you'd rule your competitive world right now and have all the customers and all the money. Face it. You're just like me. You're a commodity. A pound of nails. The only way you can win is by having the lowest price. Unless . . . you follow the very sound, very practical, very real-world advice in this book.

If you don't want to compete solely on lowest price, then join the club. I don't either. Simply put, David Avrin cuts through the nonsense and gets down to what I believe to be the absolutely essential business truths that we all need to understand to succeed and then sustain that success. You have to stand out.

For example, he writes about the power of finding your niche and being able to truthfully say, "This is what we do." I am in the business of advising companies on competitive positioning and I honestly want to rip this chapter from the book and force feed it to my clients. Yes! *This is what we do.* The power of that single concept makes this book worth many times what you paid for it. Please, please heed David's advice and do *not* try to be all things to all people.

Then I read David's take on "Ligers" and I thought, "No! Wait! *This* is the essential idea!" You'll see what Ligers are later. Suffice it to say at this point that I agree that the market leaders of the future will be Ligers. The companies that go it alone will be, well, dead meat.

Please pay particular attention to the story of the aquarium that wanted to teach people about ecosystems and how to be environmentally responsible. The owners of the aquarium were passionate about this cause and I say, good for them. It's a noble cause. The problem was that the customers were paying to be entertained, not to be indoctrinated.

I have been telling businesses and entrepreneurs for years that you can be passionate about what you do until you are crying real tears and you're red in the face, but it doesn't mean that anybody else will share your passion—and it certainly doesn't mean that people will pay you for it. If the customer isn't also passionate about what you're doing, then you don't have a business. You have a hobby.

I could rant for pages about what I think works in business, but that would take up time that you could spend more wisely reading what David has to say.

Bottom line on what I think about this book: I wish like hell that I'd written it.

Start reading.

—Joe Calloway
Author of *Becoming a Category of One*

ACKNOWLEDGMENTS

In putting together a book of wisdom, it's essential to recognize where that wisdom, experience, perspective, and hard-won knowledge were acquired.

Many of my mentors were and are the pioneering thought-leaders of the marketing world, such as Al Ries, Jack Trout, Harry Beckwith, and the amazing Joe Calloway. I've been pushed and inspired by my peers in the professional speaking world as well. From Mark Sanborn and Mark LeBlanc, to Shep Hyken, Scott McKain, Marshall Goldsmith, and the brilliant Giovanni Livera.

Thanks go to my many professional colleagues for their insights, inspiration, and friendship over the years: Sam Richter, Alan Stevens, Larry Holdren, and my best friend, mentor and mentee, Eric Chester.

Thanks to Jody Rein, my literary agent extraordinaire, for her endless wisdom and guidance through the process; to Heather Lutze for her introduction to Wiley; to Dan Ambrosio, Linda Indig, Christine Moore, and Ashley Allison, the crack team at John Wiley & Sons, for their constant encouragement and affirmation. It's been a pleasure working with true professionals and great people.

A big thanks to Janet Fogarty and my amazing colleagues at Vistage International, the world's leading CEO member organization, for their profound insight, experience, and guidance through the most fulfilling journey of my professional life. To my Vistage group members, thanks for the privilege of being your leader and coach and for allowing me to learn more about business, life, and leadership from you each month than most other professionals learn in a year.

Thank you to my precious family for your support and patience as I write yet another book. Sierra, Sydney, and Spencer, you inspire me to be more than I am, achieve more than I thought I could, and to never stop contributing to the world you will inherit.

Thanks to my amazing wife Debbie for pretending to be occasionally impressed with me, and for trying your best not to glaze-over as I read to you yet another business article I've written that has nothing whatsoever to do with your world or interests you in any way. I would die of loneliness without you.

And finally, to every client and colleague that I have ever helped, hurt, launched, inspired, frustrated, thrilled, or learned from while excelling or falling short. Thank you. I owe you, or you owe me. It is the wisdom born of those experiences that has equipped, infused. and inspired me to write this book.

INTRODUCTION (DON'T SKIP THIS!)

I don't know if this is true for you, but I always seem to run into people who think they know me from somewhere. It's excruciating as I desperately search my memory, trying to put their face or name in context, usually unsuccessfully. I tend to respond to the greeting with feigned recognition and an innocuous, "Hey! What's new and exciting in your life?" in the hope that the ensuing moments will bring a comment or reference that will provide the clue necessary to make the connection.

Of course, I'm not alone in this dynamic. We all encounter people whom we think we know. Perhaps it's the public nature of what I do for a living that causes my face and name to get out there. But the truth is that it is essential for my business success that I both preach and personify a high, public profile. My work is all about touting the benefits of becoming—and remaining—highly visible; and in expressing this message, I have to be visible as well. I would suggest that, if you are in business, the same holds true for you.

In the business world there is so much emphasis placed on the importance of networking and "who you know." While it can certainly be beneficial to develop connections with power brokers and other well-connected individuals, I'm not just playing semantics when I suggest that it's far more important to recognize the importance of who knows *you*.

Legendary sales guru Jeffrey Gitomer said it best when he coined the phrase: "*In sales, it's not who you know, in sales it's who knows you!*" I believe the same holds true in marketing and branding. The fact is that you can never know all your prospective customers, but if you're going to attract new customers or clients, they'd better know you. As I am fond of reminding my audiences: "If they don't know who you are, they can't buy what you're selling."

Recently, I was successful in securing exposure for a client's product on NBC's top-rated *Today* show. Although the segment was brief, my client's business and opportunities exploded soon afterwards. Clearly, she didn't suddenly know millions of new people as a result of her product being featured on national TV. She wouldn't know these people if she met them on the street, nor could she ring them up and connect over coffee. But they certainly know about her—or at least about her product and now her phone is ringing and ringing. Nirvana!

I was recently hired to do a presentation on strategic branding in Melbourne, Australia by a gentleman who'd heard an audio recording of a speech I gave more than six years ago. I didn't know him, and would likely have never met him, but he certainly knew me. Now, my wife and I got to meet him in person on the other side of the world—and I got paid to do it! Was it serendipity that we connected? As one of my favorite lines from the movie *The Incredibles* puts it: "Chance favors the prepared, Dahling."

Had I not presented at that conference six years ago—and put myself out there—the recording would not have been made and he wouldn't have known me from a Koala. Lucky? Maybe; but someone once said: "I am a great believer in luck; and I find the harder I work, the luckier I get!" Every time you have the opportunity to showcase your expertise, product, service, location, name, jingle, logo, or message from the stage, the big screen, small screen, Internet, radio, newspaper, webinar, billboard, soapbox, Tweet, tradeshow, podcast, or e-zine—you are reaching exponentially more people than you will ever get to know, but they will certainly have an opportunity to know you.

None of this is meant to diminish the importance of developing and fostering strong, honest, and mutually beneficial business and personal relationships. The point is that one well-placed media appearance or strategic presentation from the platform will likely trump any synergistic lunch meeting with a colleague or Facebook connection with an old flame.

You can work hard to secure a meeting with a noted CEO, or you can speak before an audience of 600 company leaders and give them first-hand exposure to your insight, wisdom, and perspective. You can do a product promotion at a local restaurant handing out samples of your new beverage, or you can hire a street team at a large festival and provide 50,000 samples. Same amount of time—very different results.

How well are you known by your prospective customers or clients right now? How many of them can you reach at a time? Knowing the right people can certainly play a big role in the success of your business, but who knows you can mean the difference between exploding sales or the end of your dream.

In this book, I explore and present numerous strategies and tactics intended to help you take a few steps back and look at your business as your customers do. In reading about how some have succeeded while others have fallen short, I hope that you will see glimpses of your own business in the examples, and be inspired to dig deep and discover your points of differentiation. It's not a traditional how-to book, and it is not presented in a linear fashion, but rather as snippets of wisdom designed to wake you up, give you pause, and at times kick your butt.

From time to time you may come across a suggestion or admonition that was mentioned at another point in the book. This is not an oversight, but a reinforcement of an important concept or caution. It is repeated only because it bears repeating.

Forget what your teachers, parents, and librarians taught you as a kid, and write all over this book! Dog-ear the pages, make notes in the margins, and highlight the heck out of it. But most important, truly consider the questions being asked and heed the counsel provided. I promise that with knowledge will come power—the power to envision, craft, build, refine, and promote a uniquely differentiated brand.

Let's go get some business!

David Avrin—The Visibility Coach

The Path to Visibility: Part 1 – Your Brand

SECTION

1

Your Brand

Who You Are
How You Arrive
How You Are Remembered

Your Brand Is . . . Everything

When it comes to building a successful business, your brand is everything—literally. It is everything you do and everything you don't do. It is the smell of your lobby and the color of your menu. It is the friendliness of your staff and their response to customer problems. It is the quality of your widgets, the timeliness of your bill paying, and the cleanliness of your bathrooms. It's how you arrive and how you depart.

Too many in today's business environment think that their brand consists primarily of their logo and their clever tag line, but a brand is so much more. In fact, it is everything. And despite your impact and influence over your brand, in the end you don't really own it. Your brand resides in the mind of your customers. Your brand is the images, thoughts, recollections, and emotions that come to people's mind when they hear your name, see your ad, or pass your store. Your brand is what your customers think, remember, and feel about your business and doing business with you—even after you've left the building.

If I were to say the words: Wal-Mart, Harley-Davidson, Cinnabon, or Pepto-Bismol—the thoughts that pop into your mind are the qualities that comprise their brands. If they've done a good job promoting their business, delivering quality goods and services, and generally living up to their word, then the images that we all share are likely very similar. Conversely, if a company falls short in any of those areas, a very different image comes to mind. That gap between a brand's promise and the consumer's perception of reality can translate into a weak brand and potential trouble for the company's future.

For some other well-known brands, consistency is only important as it relates to their target market. These companies and organizations don't try to be all things to all people, but for their core audiences their brand drives their business. From *Playboy*, MTV, and the National Rifle Association, to Greenpeace, Focus on the Family, and *Marlboro Cigarettes*, these organizations clearly know their audience and tailor their products and messaging to that group. If you don't agree with the company's stance, then you are not in their target market.

So, as you look at your business, ask yourself these three important questions:

1. Is my product, service, environment, look, feel, and smell truly unique?

2. Am I consistent in delivering on the promise—every time?

3. Is my business memorable—for all the right reasons?

Never forget that you and your brand are always on stage and that someone is always watching, listening, evaluating, and deciding whom to buy from. Craft your brand, ensuring that the process is in place to deliver the right message to the right audience consistently. Then—and *only* then—should you invite people in.

Visibility COACH The Visibility Coach says: We have no control over our brand—but we have great influence.

How Do You Arrive?

I called a potential vendor the other day, and was taken aback by what I heard on the other end of the phone. In fact, I was so stunned that I forgot who I was calling or why. What began as a simple telephone call shifted to surprise and bewilderment, then quickly to utter disbelief and annoyance. "Could this really be happening?" I asked myself. I hung up the phone pondering whether to call back, or just move on to another potential supplier.

Instead, I dialed again and motioned for my six-year-old son to come into my office. As I put the telephone receiver to his ear so he could listen to the repeating tone of the busy signal so familiar to us "old people," a puzzled look came over his face. I asked him if he knew what the sound meant. He

head and then shrugged, saying rather matter-
"It means it's broken."

As far as I am concerned, the potential business with that vendor is indeed broken. I've moved on. Now, you may be thinking to yourself that perhaps the phone line was down, or other technical difficulties caused the busy signal. My response: it doesn't matter. I've moved on. I don't have time to waste trying to call them back later. I need to get my work done, and alternatives are plentiful.

The same holds true if your neighbor relays a bad experience she had at a local eatery, or you arrive at a retail store right at closing time and the employees won't let you in, or an annoying radio jingle haunts you, or you pull a business card from your pocket and can't remember from the poorly designed card who they are or what they do. Are you going to spend time trying to figure out the answers and give them a second chance? Not likely. You are too busy. We're all too busy, and there are too many other businesses that do a better job. You just move on.

The lesson: In an age of almost limitless choices, first impressions are more crucial now than they have ever been. How you arrive matters.

Your brand—and the likelihood that others will do business with you—is determined in large part by first impressions. Yes, my friends, you've heard it before: Business is like high school. People do work with people and companies that they like, so they had better like you right away! Your brand is everything others see, hear, smell, learn, and remember—and everything they don't. First impressions don't simply matter; most often, they will determine whether you even get up to bat.

So—what first impression are you giving your customers and prospective clients? I'm not simply referring to your front-line greeting delivered over the phone or at the front counter. This includes every possible way a prospect learns about you and your business—from the look and feel of your location entrance, the clarity of your business offering on your web site home page and your frontline staff's attitude, to the originality of your name and logo, the positive or negative press you receive, the pithiness of your slogan, and the tales told by past customers. It all matters—a lot!

One of the most difficult things you will ever do in your business is change a first impression. Once a feeling is felt, a complaint from a friend is heard, an experience is . . . well . . . experienced, it is a monumental task to try to undo that impression. That's why so often you will see a banner outside a recently purchased retail business that says: *Under New Management.* What they're really saying is: "You might have had a bad experience before, but now we're different!" Tough chore.

When was the last time you did an "experience audit"—on yourself? Have you tried to call your own business to see how long it takes to get out of voice-menu hell if you were calling for the first time? Have you surveyed your current and past clients to truly learn what you did well or how you fell short in their eyes? Do you use a mystery shopping service or get feedback from people who don't know what your employee manual says?

The challenge is to step back, take the time to look at all the touch points of your business, and ask these questions: Does this method of learning about my business say what I want to say—and what my customers want to hear? Is it easy to reach me, clear what I do, and make the case for hiring me over my competition? Does my business look good, smell great, and is it impeccably clean and presentable? Are my business proposition and differentiating factors crystal clear and memorable (in the right way)? Am I creating a new ambassador with every encounter? Do I come across as arrogant or affable, approachable and credible? In short, do prospective customers like me right away?

The "busy" vendor I hung up on yesterday will never even know that I was trying to reach them. Their loss.

Too often, you never even know what potential business you lose by a poorly executed first moment with a prospect. Don't leave it to chance. Analyze, correct, train, execute, and continually reevaluate your touch points.

Visibility COACH   The Visibility Coach says: First impressions matter—a lot!

An Inch Wide and a Mile Deep

What are you good at? Let me rephrase that question: What are you so darned good at that nobody does it better?

Many of my prospective clients come to me with a laundry list of subjects about which they speak, write, consult or provide services for. I ask where their expertise truly lies, and they show me a long list. Then they are often taken aback when I tell them that I wouldn't hire them to help me with any subject on their list.

I go on to explain that while they may be extremely insightful in every area listed, there is already some professional who promotes themselves as the "guru" in each one of those subjects. Why should I trust someone who is a self-described expert on so many subjects when I can hire an expert who specializes in just the area I need? These people must be good, I think, because that's all they do!

In his popular book *Selling the Invisible*, Harry Beckwith talks about the mistaken belief that people try to make the best decision possible in their purchases. The reality is that most people are trying to avoid making a bad decision. They opt for "good" over the promise of "great," if that promise carries risk. A jack-of-all-trades is risky. A specialist is not.

So I ask the question again. What are you *darned* good at?

Many business people worry that they are leaving money on the table if they narrow their focus. "If I can offer more products and services to my customers, then I'll make more money," they assume. In some cases it is true, but it depends on how far from the core brand they are venturing. The truth is that many diverse businesses make far less money, because they are out-of-the-running for most prospective customers before they even begin to pitch. The services or products they market are too broad. The specialist gets the call, and often the business as well.

As a rule, the marketplace celebrates specialists and often bypasses the generalist. Where do you want to go to lunch today—the First National Savings, Loan, and Salad Bar, or Soup-N-Salad? Who do you want to hardwire your new, state-of-the-art, multi-million-dollar office building—a local handyman or a well-known electrical contractor?

Generalists may be cheaper, but carry risk. Specialists are a safer choice.

I have many professional speaker colleagues who provide a list of their individual specialties, such as Leadership, Change, Customer Service, Motivation, Corporate Culture, Stress, Diversity, Humor, and Time Management. No matter what you need, they are willing to speak on it.

Now, be honest, if you needed to hire a speaker on diversity in the workplace, would you hire someone who also speaks on internet search marketing? Of course not. You'd find someone that specializes in helping companies deal with diversity issues. And moreover, you'd probably find someone who also wrote a book on the subject.

You need to be *the one*—or at least the first one—that comes to mind in your unique area.

Visibility COACH   The Visibility Coach says: Be a Specialist. Find your niche and promote your specific expertise.

The Four Most Dangerous Words in Business

For those of us in business, danger lurks around every corner. From rapidly changing market conditions, to the impact of terrorism, and even unscrupulous employees, work is called work for a reason—it's hard out there!

But there are four words that should strike terror into the hearts of anyone seeking to compete in the marketplace: four small words that, when arranged in a certain order, can cast doubt on your very ability to remain in business. Perhaps you're thinking of something along the lines of "Dateline NBC is outside!" or "The building is burning!" Perhaps "We are being audited" or "Our patent got declined."

The truth is, there are endless negative business scenarios that can be boiled down to only four words, but most are unlikely to happen—at least to you. However, when it comes to positioning your business or service, the four most dangerous words are: "All things being equal."

When applied to your business, that phrase should stop you dead in your tracks because it signifies that you've failed to distinguish yourself from your competitors. It means that you've merely thrown yourself out there and left it to others to determine if you are worthy of selection. If you offer essentially (and don't quibble with me about the meaning of "essentially") the same product or service as your competitors, and there's nothing to clearly distinguish you, then their choice will likely be based on chance, proximity, or worse yet—price!

Pizza, for example has become a commodity. While there are some exceptional pizzas out there—and most have engaging marketing programs—the truth is that most delivered pizza is chosen by one simple criterion: All things being equal, most buy the pizza that matches the coupon they find in the junk drawer. How would you like your revenue totals largely determined by who has the better coupon that week? Ouch!

The reality is that if you want to be a market leader, you simply can't *allow* all things to be equal. You *must* gain an advantage. Whether merely perceived by your prospects, or truly demonstrated through your superior skills or product—*you* must be the better choice. You cannot allow yourself to be seen as equivalent to your competitors.

Perhaps you stand out with your clearly superior products, more engaging marketing campaign, simple and easy-to-navigate web site, much higher profile, or remarkable customer service. Whatever it is, you must be better at something—and be known for what sets you apart.

Seniors have long struggled with childproof lids on medication bottles, yet nothing had changed for decades until Target® stores introduced the ClearRx®, a redesigned prescription bottle and label to make it easier for seniors to take their medication. Nordstrom has built a reputation for having the best retail return policy. Westin Hotels feature the Heavenly® Bed (and yes, it's that good). The new Virgin American Airlines gives every passenger power ports and multifunction screens at every seat (and at the same price as other airlines' basic seats). And Apple has . . . well, Apple has done everything differently.

Even in traditional commodity categories such as eggs and milk, companies have found ways to transcend their category and stand out. EggLand's Best® infuses the feed their chickens eat with higher levels of Omega 3. Lactaid® brand milk provides milk to those suffering from lactose intolerance. And even those who turned the ultimate commodity, water, into a brand, have found ways to further stand apart by including flip-top lids and more ergonomic shapes for the bottles.

When most in your industry offer essentially the same promise, opportunities abound to set yourself apart. Although you can't control a prospect's personal preferences, you can do a better job of zeroing in on their problems, offer more creative solutions, or make yourself more visible.

So, do more than just offer yourself as another entry in the race. Sweeten the pot, up the ante, and grab the chance to step up and shine. Conduct more extensive research into what your clients want and need—and then deliver it. Offer value-added services and creative extras that your competition would have never thought of. Raise your credibility (and their comfort level) with successful case studies and positive press coverage. In positioning yourself, lead with something unique that your competitors can't claim (or wished they'd thought of first). In short, make it difficult for clients *not* to choose you.

Remember: your prospects always have choices. All things being equal, they can easily choose someone else. But if you stand out, stand apart, and become the clear choice, you'll likely get the business—and your price!

Visibility COACH   The Visibility Coach says: Don't ever let everything be equal—ever!

Schtick Out!

Pop quiz time! Grab a number 2 pencil (remember those?) and connect the person to the buzz word, tag line, or signature activity:

Created the Weiner-Mobile

Invented the "Moon Walk"

Rude *American Idol* judge

Undersea documentary filmmaker

Invented the first instant camera and film

(continued)

(*Continued*)

Heiress party-girl

Comedian who famously complained: "*I don't get no respect*"

Shock-Jock

Created the Muppets

Manic fitness evangelist running around in tiny striped jogging shorts

First man to walk on the moon (the first *real* Moon Walk!)

Did you think that was too easy? Good. That's the point. I could have crafted a very challenging list of obscure and hard-to-peg individuals, with dubious distinctions or hard-to-recall accomplishments, but I really don't care about those people—and you shouldn't either. The fact of the matter is that if your signature schtick, catchphrase, claim to fame, or clever moniker is hard to remember and doesn't point to you, then you've missed the mark.

To become top-of-mind, you need to craft or highlight something about yourself, your message, or your business that is readily and easily identifiable with you—and *only* you. When you hear someone say, "Yah, it's been done," it's usually a not very subtle reminder that there is nothing special in copying someone else. So here's the question: What do you do, that only you do?

Here are some current examples of people who have expertly crafted a signature activity or message. I offer them not as examples to be copied, but rather as inspiration:

- You may not know the name Judson Laipply, but chances are you've seen his video. "The Evolution of Dance" is a monster hit on YouTube and has been passed around the country like wildfire. In fact, his is the most viewed video on YouTube; as of this writing, the video has been viewed online nearly 200 million times! Laipply is a corporate, college, and high school speaker, and he just wanted to create something entertaining to finish out his program. This finish has taken him to the *Today* show, Oprah, Ellen DeGeneres, and more. Many others have copied it, but it's *his* schtick. Brilliant!

- Others have tried to coin a term for the emerging generation of confusing, complex, and often frustrating young people just coming of age and entering the workforce. Monikers such as Millenials, Gen Y, Echo Boomers, the Me-Too Generation, Nexters, and others were thrown around in articles and books. It wasn't until Eric Chester coined the term "Generation Why" that it truly became part of the public lexicon. A reporter recently sent out a query to PR firms across America looking for an expert on young workers and the consternation that they were causing employers. She received dozens of responses— and every single one of them suggested she talk to Eric Chester. Any doubt he owns the brand?

- Singapore has a reputation for being remarkably clean— and it is.

- Doubletree Hotels feature their legendary chocolate chip cookies.

- Volvo makes the safest cars in the world.

- Michael Jackson wore his signature white glove.

- Robin Williams always delivers manic and over-the-top media interviews.
- Johnny Cash always wore black.
- Madonna constantly reinvents herself.
- Disney's young stars are always squeaky-clean, and conservative political commentator Ann Coulter is intentionally provocative and controversial.

Sports has its share of signature schtick as well:

- LeBron James always throws talcum powder in the air before a game.
- Golfer Chi Chi Rodriguez wields his golf club like a sword.
- Olympic swimming gold medalist Amy Van Dyken spits into her opponent's lane prior to a race.
- Sportscaster John Madden hasn't stepped on an airplane since 1979, instead opting to ride his bus dubbed the Madden Cruiser.

It's their shtick. It's what they do, and if well-established over time, it's what becomes part of their identity. Anyone who tries to copy them will likely look foolish.

Some people are actually best known for their body parts. Dolly Parton and Pamela Anderson played up their bust size. Jennifer Lopez emphasizes her back side. Jay Leno makes fun of his own big chin. Thirty years ago Arnold muscled his way to stardom, while Twiggy was, well, twiggy.

So, what are you known for? If there are others who profess to offer the marketplace something similar to you and your business—how do you "schtick out?" What query would generate your name as the response? In other words, to what question are *you* the answer?

The takeaway: To become well known you have to be . . . well, *known* for something! So look at your gifts and your quirks, and latch onto something clever and creative. Create or craft something that is memorable and applies only to you. Then, guard it with your career.

Visibility COACH   The Visibility Coach says: Be original. Be memorable and be known for your own Schtick.

Who Do the Voodoo?

How many people or businesses are in your category? If the answer is "quite a few," then you'd better be darned good at what you do if you want to compete in a category that many others are fighting to dominate. If you are struggling for market share (assuming that you're priced competitively), then you've likely got one or more of three problems:

1. You aren't as good as you think.
2. You haven't clearly differentiated yourself from your competitors.
3. You are being out-marketed and out-promoted.

If you come to realize after looking at yourself honestly and objectively that the answer is #1, then my advice is to get out of the business. Seriously. Either get better, or go do something else. Of course, there are always some tricks you can use to help you pretend you are better than you are, but I'm not going to be the one to help you figure them out, and you'll ultimately be discovered anyway.

If the answer is #2, then you need try to discover and clarify what you can be the best at. It may be some small facet of your business, but it has to be something. Maybe all you really need is to draw a distinction.

One good strategy is to recognize that there are aspects of every profession or business with which some clients or customers are generally dissatisfied. Take that item of dissatisfaction and address it in your business model and your marketing. Correct it in your product or service, and then brag about your unique solution.

While peanut butter and jelly sandwiches have long been a staple in kids' school lunches, the jelly would often make the bread soggy long before the school's lunch hour. Smucker's® found a way to surround the jelly on all sides with peanut butter and tuck them both in a pocket of bread—without the crust! The popularity of Uncrustables® was easy to predict.

If your struggle is with being out-marketed and out-promoted, then forget the old adage "don't work harder, just work smarter." In reality, you have to do both. But the good news is that there is no need to recreate the wheel. There is a wealth of creative and effective promotional ideas from books, speakers, case-studies, competitors, and peers. Try approaches from within and outside your industry. Be creative and try new approaches.

The takeaway: Marketing is not a department. Everyone in your organization has a marketing role—but you must be on the same page. Be creative. Be persistent. Be strategic. Be smart. Be visible!

Visibility COACH   The Visibility Coach says: Never stop evaluating and making adjustments.

What's in a Name?

Million-dollar product—ten-cent name? Too many companies today—both large and small—are making the mistake of putting all their time and talent into their product or service itself and far too little into its name. It can very difficult to build a brand around the National General Corporation, Paradigm Industries, Dynamic Trucking, or the Preferred Dairy Company. All sound generic, nondescript, and boring.

I see it in my industry as well; too many professional speakers and consultants go to market with company names like Leadership Strategies, Team Builders, Change Managers, or (fill in the name) Speaks! Descriptive names such as these do nothing to highlight your specific or creative approach, create a memorable impression, or differentiate you from your competition.

On the other hand, many professionals make the mistake of being overly clever with names that have tremendous personal meaning to the business owner, but that mean nothing to their intended marketplace. I knew a woman who named her publishing company "Laika" after her cat. Too many name products and companies after their kids. Some will use the names of mythical figures like; Helios, Artemis, Poseidon,

Ceres, or Thor. Others make up words like Provenent, Exempla, and Innovous. Then there are companies named Dynamus, Dynimus, Dynamos, and Dynamous, These are hard to remember and even harder to spell. Far too many others simply use their initials or those of their children, such as DLA Consultants or PQR Publishing.

I'm not suggesting that names such as these cannot be successful; many have been. But for every success story, there are thousands of missteps or outright failures.

One of the best examples of the made-up name is Haagen-Dazs. It sounds so foreign and exotic. The name was originally envisioned by reversing the name of Duncan Hines (*Huncan-Dines*), one of the original potential marketers of the ice cream. When that deal didn't materialize, the name was manipulated to look and sound Scandinavian.

I've talked with many proud company owners who regale me with the story of how the name for their product or organization came to be. I've received history lessons, linguistic tutoring on how to pronounce their name, and unwanted insights into the individual's genetic lineage and affection for their pets. Why? What does this have to do with your customers?

Remember this: If your name requires an explanation, then you've just shot yourself in the foot. You can still walk if you're darned good at what you do—it's just going to be a lot harder and take far more time to get where you are going.

If you had the opportunity to do it over again—or you have the opportunity to begin something new—you will save yourself a great deal of time and money down the road by investing your time and resources to do it the right way now.

A company or product name, seminar title, or business moniker should begin the process of educating your prospects. It should, in a memorable, clever, or creative way, give a sense of who you are and what you offer. Literal names are rarely successful. Think of the Internet. How many times have you visited books.com, searchengine.com, or auctions.com? However, I have no doubt you've spent significant time on Amazon, Google, and eBay.

Does your moniker say something about you, your audience, your market, what you offer, and what you believe? Or are you just so enamored with your own initials that you think they create a memorable and descriptive company name?

___

Visibility COACH   The Visibility Coach says: When you craft the name for your business, product, or service, give it the same consideration and attention that you would in naming your own baby—because in a way, that's what you are doing.

___

Tag—You're It!

Much has been written about the importance of crafting the right company name, the perfect product moniker, or an inspiring, professional title. But equally important—and often short-changed—is a creative, memorable, and impacting tagline. While your company name, your logo, and service mark are the public face of who you are, the tagline should tell people what you do, who you do it for, and why you are different from your competition. Like peanut butter and jelly, both can be darned good on their own, but put 'em together—magic!

Unfortunately, people get lazy and creativity gives way to expediency. In recent years, the marketplace has experienced a rash of very poorly considered—but likely very expensive—campaigns that push meaningless and forgettable taglines. Inexcusable! Most of these ill-conceived messages undoubtedly make a great deal of money for the high-priced ad agencies, but they do little for the client or their sales.

In agency conference rooms and company boardrooms, executives fall all over each other with self-congratulations, thinking they've invented the cure for cancer that tastes like chocolate with their simple assertions. But in reality, most have simply added another forgettable, nonspecific message to the mix. In their quest to be different and clever, most forget the most important element: that the message must make the product or company stand out and lead to actual sales!

A well-crafted tagline should clarify, in a creative way, the target market, what makes the product or company different, and how it applies to the customer. Harder still, it must be done in very few words. For some, it's only a word or two; for others it's a simple sentence or profound declaration.

Some of the more innocuous entries either say nothing special, something unintended, or make a promise that consumers don't believe. Too many waste a golden opportunity by using meaningless superlatives like better, best, great, outstanding, unique, and excellent so commonly that they've lost their impact. Contrary to its name, "unique" just isn't anymore.

One of the most worthless and overused terms is the word "solutions"—not only because it has it lost its punch through sheer overuse, but because the term has been hijacked by the IT industry. Some of the worst words currently in use are detailed in a terrific article in *Advertising Age* by Stephen Winzenburg. http://adage.com/cmostrategy/article?article_id= 122982

The lion's share of meaningless taglines fail the most obvious test: Do the words truly describe the company or product or can the slogan be lifted and inserted under the name of a competitor? Or worse yet, would it apply to almost any company in any industry? You can try to convince us that "Our People Make the Difference," but so do the people in virtually every company in every industry.

Some notably bad taglines include:

- Mazda—*Zoom. Zoom.* (Does this make you want to buy their cars? Don't all cars go Zoom, Zoom?)
- Bud Light—*The Difference is Drinkability* (Don't you hate those other beverages that are difficult to drink?)
- Avis—*We Try Harder* (Not really bad, but the original tagline was much better: *"We're Number 2—We Try Harder!"* It was an acknowledgment of how the second place competitor will often do much more to earn its way to the top. The current, abbreviated version says nothing that everyone else doesn't say).
- Dodge—*It's a New Day!* (It's kind of like saying: "I know we used to be kind of bad, but now we've started over.")
- BDO Seidman—*"People who know, know BDO."* (I don't have any idea who you are or what you do, but apparently somebody does.)
- UPS—*What can brown do for you?* (Unfortunately, the 12-year-old boy in me comes out and I have to just hold my tongue.)

- Yoplait Yogurt—*Together, we can lick breast cancer.* (Um, Honey . . . did they just say "lick breast cancer?" No, seriously, did they?)

- McDonald's—*I'm Lovin' it!* (Great song, but honestly, does anybody older than seven really *love* McDonald's? Better was: *"Did somebody say McDonald's?* It said, "On the spur of the moment, this is an easy choice." Which is what McDonald's is: fast, easy, and pretty good. But sorry, I'm not "Lovin' it.")

- U.S. Army—*An Army of One.* (Okay . . . Then who's got your back?)

- Ford—*Bold Moves* (What does this say about quality, differentiation, innovation, fun . . . ?)

- Sears—*Where it begins* (I'm speechless.)

Some of the best include:

- The *Wall Street Journal—The Daily Diary of the American Dream* (So good, it gives me chills!)

- Monster.com—*Your Calling is Calling* (It's not just a job—but your true calling. Brilliant!)

- *Maxim* magazine—*The Best Thing to Happen to Men—Since Women!* (The perfect message for their target market. If this tag offends you, then you aren't the target market.)

- Rogaine—*Use it or Lose it!* (Perfect use of a well-worn phrase. Also lays out the scenario of what will happen if you fail to use their product.)

- Friends of the Earth—*Think Globally, Act Locally* (A future hall-of-famer. What to do, and how to do it.)

- RTW (workers compensation insurance)—*Transforming People From Absent or Idle, to Present and Productive* (They can take your limping slackers and transform them into walking workers. Sold!)

- Secret—*Because You're Hot!* (A great double-entendre, and one of the best of the new breed.)

- The Home Depot—*You can do it. We can help!* (Their real competition is not Lowe's, it's handymen and contractors—or not doing it at all. This offer of encouragement addresses that choice head-on.)

- Lay's Potato Chips—*Betcha can't eat just one!* (Not just a testament to how good they are, but a challenge as well! You're on!)

- FedEx—*When it Absolutely, Positively Has to Be There Overnight* (Is there any other reason to use and pay for overnight shipping? A hall-of-famer indeed!)

- Disneyland—*The Happiest Place on Earth!* (Unless you've got a 5-year-old who hasn't had a nap.)

- Berlitz—*Immerse and Converse* (Foreign-language system whose tag says: "If you do this, you can do that. Couldn't be clearer.)

- The E! Entertainment Network's True Hollywood Story—*Because there's no such thing as TMI.* (We like dirty laundry.)

- The Visibility Coach—*It's Not Who You Know—It's Who Knows YOU!* ('Nuff said.)

- And my all-time favorite: Head and Shoulders—*Because You Never Get a Second Chance to Make a First Impression.*

Don't shortchange the process! Spend as much time, effort, and resources on crafting a truly profound, marketable, and memorable tagline as you do on the name and logo. Challenge your own words. Could they describe almost anyone, or is the verbiage unique to you and your business? Remember that consumers always have a choice in the marketplace and you need to get and keep their attention to be considered. If your tagline is generic, prospects will think you are just another player. This isn't easy, but it's worth every hour you put into it!

Visibility COACH   The Visibility Coach says: If your tagline is forgettable, customers will forget you. It's time to take a good hard look at what you say and how you say it.

No, Wait. Come Back!

Very few businesses can survive and thrive without the all-important repeat customer. Some studies suggest that it can cost up to ten times as much to attract a first time customer than to keep a customer you already have, so it behooves you to give them a reason to return.

Now to be clear, this isn't going to be a lesson on customer service. We all know the basics: Say what you'll do and do what you say. Treat the customer well. Meet or exceed their expectations, etc. There are plenty of books, speakers, consultants, articles, and so on that will remind us how to deliver on the promise.

But what happens when there is a fundamental disconnect between the promise and the delivery? What happens when the intent of the seller and the desire of the customer fail to connect? Too often, a customer's first visit is their last.

When a new Brazilian restaurant promises a high-energy international flair—but instead you find gum-chewing teens serving up meat in a converted Bennigan's—you're not likely to return. Even if the food is good, the expectations were not met and there are others in the market who do it better.

There are too many individuals in business today who think the most important thing to do is to follow your heart and heed the inspirational adage that says: "Do what you love and the money will follow." But it doesn't always work out that way. Just because you want to say something doesn't mean that others want to hear it, or that you have the ability to deliver it. Just because you've discovered that your passion is to make or sell something doesn't mean that customers will love it as you do, or pay money for it.

Fans of the show *American Idol* witness this dynamic every season. Out of the vast catalogue of potential song choices, many an aspiring singer will opt for a song that "means a great deal to me," as they say. It could be a song that touches their heart, or is their mom's favorite ballad and they are singing it for her. But the judges continually remind that this is a competition, and if the song doesn't touch the audience the same way it does dear old Mom, the contestant loses.

Business is very much the same way. Your words, product offering, and other marketplace entries have to satisfy both your passion and the customers desire or need. If push comes to shove, opt for their need and satisfy your passion in some other way.

In the late 1990s, there was a push to build an aquarium in Denver, Colorado. Being land-locked, Denver was hardly known for its abundant marine life, but that was the rallying cry for supporters of the endeavor. People in the middle states had little exposure to the wonders of the ocean and this could be a great way to bring the ocean to the mountains. Led by a husband and wife team of marine biologists, a consortium of public and private entities came together to build the largest aquarium from Los Angeles to Chicago.

When the doors opened on June 21, 1999 near downtown Denver, the crowds were huge and the lines were long. It seems as if they did everything right. The marketing campaign and news media coverage dominated the airwaves. The building was stunning. Beautiful tanks were filled with amazing sea life from around the world, and even live Sumatran tigers had their place in the above-water ecosystem displays.

I was a part of that crowd as my wife and I took our kids through the exhibit during the opening week. About 15 minutes into the journey, I turned to my wife and said: "They will be out of business within two years."

Why? Because it became abundantly clear that the founders' vision was being realized. They wanted to teach us about ecosystems. They wanted us to understand how important it was that we protect and conserve. They wanted us to know what we, as humans, are doing to destroy our planet and the marine life within it. What they forgot to ask—or didn't even care about—was what *we* wanted and were willing pay for. We thought we were buying entertainment; they were on a mission to change our way of thinking. They went bankrupt in April of 2002.

At a total cost to build of $93 million, Colorado Ocean Journey was purchased by Landry's Seafood House for $13.6 million. Today, reconfigured for entertainment and known as the Downtown Aquarium (with seafood restaurant inside), it flourishes.

The lesson: Step back and look at your business to see if you've struck that balance. I'm all for being passionate about what you do, but ensure that you are clear on what your potential customers and clients want. Then deliver that.

Visibility COACH The Visibility Coach says: Deliver what your customers actually want, and they'll come back. Do it better than your competition and they'll come back again and again.

Your Personality Is Your Brand

There is no more apparent demonstration of professional personality than in the outward expression of what we, as business owners, believe and stand for. But of course, everyone has beliefs and opinions. And more than ever before, we have seemingly endless avenues for sharing our opinions with anyone willing to listen. Just look at the airwaves, the Internet, and the newsstand. From call-in talk shows and other broadcast gab-fests, to e-zines, chat rooms, MySpace, Facebook, Twitter, YouTube, and the explosion of Internet blogs, everyone has something to say—and they're fighting to get their voice heard.

The glut of voices creates even greater challenges for organizations and professionals looking to build and promote their brand in the marketplace. Too many in business are looking to differentiate themselves by discovering the secret formula for getting the microphone or camera turned in their direction. Well, I hate to break it to you—but there isn't a secret formula. The answer is right in front of you—on the air, online, and in newspaper columns across America every day. You just have to pay attention and recognize the source of the music.

What is the common personality characteristic shared by Al Sharpton, Nancy Grace, Bill O'Reilly, Dr. Laura, Richard Simmons, Steve Jobs, Dennis Miller, Oprah Winfrey, Ron Paul, and even anti-war protestor Cindy Sheehan? (Before you assert that they represent a level of annoyance, remember that one person's static is a symphony to another.) The answer is that they are all on a very public and passionate crusade. They have a personal mission, and they're shouting it from the rooftops. Moreover, each one has honed his or her message and by doing so they communicate their personality clearly, concisely, and consistently. They stay on message and look for any opportunity to espouse their beliefs or make their case to an audience. They bolster their message by tying current events and hot news stories to their subject. And above all, they have strong opinions and don't mince words. They don't say: "Here's the subject; what do you think?" They tell you what they believe and you are free to agree or disagree.

Developing and marketing a dynamic business personality follows the same formula. There is no mistaking the personality of such business greats as Ben & Jerry's, Nordstrom, Google, The Ritz Carlton, Chuck-E-Cheese, Virgin Airlines, and Apple. It's more than simply espousing and promoting a business philosophy or organizational message. These highly differentiated and unique companies are consistently walking the walk as well as talking the talk. They live the message in everything they do—and everything they don't do.

They are on a crusade for innovation, customer service, community service, luxury, fun or fitness. It's more than an approach; it's a mission, and their personality is always on display.

But it's important to avoid confusing a strong opinion with a credible crusade and an engaging personality. The qualities that differentiate between the messages that get heard and those that don't are the embodiment of three distinct qualities: relevance, credibility, and passion. This triumvirate is the three-legged stool that companies need to stand upon in order to make it to the big media stage.

Time for a gut check: Does your crusade pass these tests? Expertise aside—are you really differentiated, opinionated, and bold enough to compete for the throne in your category? Are you speaking to a niche market, or have you found the hook to create a relevant and captivating persona to a broad audience?

Here's a test: You have a TV camera pointed at your face. You have 90 seconds to say everything about your subject, your passion, and crusade that you've been dying to get off your chest. In your perfect world, what needs to happen or change? What have others consistently gotten wrong that you have addressed and corrected in your business? You need to fill the entire 90 uninterrupted seconds with relevant, passionate, and articulate points that excite people and move them to action. Ready? Go.

Could you do it? If not, dog-ear this page, close the book, turn off your cell phone, close your door, and put pen to paper. It's more than an elevator speech; it's what you'd scream from the top of the mountain if you got there. One short elevator speech gets you a business card. The other puts you on the road to revealing your unique personality to the broad marketplace and becoming top-of-mind with your top prospects.

Visibility COACH   The Visibility Coach says: To make it to the big media stage, crank up your expertise and passion, and bring your engaging business personality to the masses.

This Is What We Do!

The last thing that any of us wants to do is leave money on the table. Right? In order to capture as much business from our clients as we can, we broaden our range of service and bring on additional expertise, or sell ancillary products to take advantage of any need our clients or customers might have.

"I need someone who can build us an XX," our prospect says.

"We can do that," we reply.

"But can you also provide us with YY?" they ask.

"Sure, we can do that too," we eagerly respond—recognizing the big payday ahead.

"Wow, really? Can you also"—"Yes," we jump in eagerly.

The answer is always: "Yes!" But wait—what was the question again? In our eagerness to capture additional business, we love to show our clients that we are smart and comprehensive, with far-reaching capabilities. What we are too often also doing is inadvertently reducing the likelihood that they will do business with us at all. In our zeal to show our vast capabilities, we merely prove that we are just like everyone else—jack-of-all, and potentially master-of-none. Translation; we are risky.

It's the neighborhood construction guy that can do everything from building you a deck, finishing your basement, fixing your toilet, and cleaning your gutters. Oh, and he can knock off 20 percent and two weeks if you just trust him and skip the permits. If you wanted your basement finished—and done correctly—wouldn't you gravitate toward a company that focused its attention and marketing efforts on basements alone?

If you've been bothered your entire life by the size and shape of your nose, there are countless plastic surgeons who could do the work and likely do it well. But if your baby was born with a cleft palate, does it still not really matter who you turn to? I would suggest it matters very much. Do you trust your child to the doctor who advertises his dramatic before and after breast augmentations, or the reconstructive surgeon who travels to third-world countries to repair cleft palates on impoverished children? Both physicians certainly *can* perform the procedure; but for one, this is *what he does*.

When you look at your business, what separates you from others who claim to offer the same products or services?

"But we're better," you might say.

"Bunk!" I reply. Your customers only know what they know, and they assume that most who claim to be competent actually are. What will make you stand out to them?

Once again, it's the specialist that truly stands apart. The market leaders who have gained a competitive advantage

often have found a vertical market niche, an industry to specialize in and a method of doing or promoting their business
that sets them apart.

How many times have we seen—but rarely actually dined
at—the restaurant that offers Italian, Mexican, Greek, *and*
American food? Their strategy clearly is: "No matter what
they are hungry for, they can find it here! It's brilliant!" they
say to themselves. And while there are sporadic examples
of success with this approach, by and large *most* fail to ever
gain traction. Why? Because there are too many other restaurant choices.

With the United Nations approach to dining, there is
always a sneaking suspicion that, with so many ethnic options
at one restaurant, the food likely isn't very good in any of the
ethnic versions. If I'm hungry for Mexican food, I'll go to a
Mexican restaurant. Why not? The food must be good at a
neighborhood Mexican restaurant, I reason, because that's all
they serve there. And usually, the predominantly ethnic staff
lends additional credibility and authenticity. Who better
than a person of Chinese descent with a Chinese family to
know what good Chinese food should taste like?

But creating confidence in your buyer is more than simply
touting a capability, it's asserting a leading role. While others
may say, "We can do that," market leaders will remind us,
"This is what we do."

For example, most web design firms boast that they can do
everything from layout, design, and functionality, to search-
engine optimization, incorporation of social media, and even
managing your Podcasting. While it's certainly smart to have
a broad array of capabilities, what then separates you from the
thousands of other companies that tout the same capabilities?

Price? Yikes! Who really wants to be the "low-cost leader?" Not me.

Web development firm Oniracom, based in Santa Barbara, California, is populated by an eclectic mix of casually dressed, twenty-something, slightly Bohemian, environmentally friendly, cyber-geeks (and I say that with all affection). They have assembled much of the same broad-range, leading-edge, Web development capabilities claimed by others in their space. The difference is that they specialize in creating a Web presence and online fan connection for music groups and rock bands. They love music and this is what they do. In fact, they have created web sites and fan-based social media integration and capabilities for top music performers such as Jack Johnson, the Counting Crowes, John Legend, The Wailers, Lenny Kravitz, Robert Cray, and Brushfire Records.

If a major record label or management company were to approach most Web firms and asked them if they could create a "killer web site" for their artists, what do you expect the response to be?

"We certainly can!" they will reply. The leaders at Oniracom, by contrast, will simply smile and say confidently: "This is what we do." They will then go on to show the broad portfolio of musician web site and promotional efforts they have created.

In a head-to-head competition, who do you think the music exec is going to go with? It's not even a question. Why take a chance? There is way too much on the line. It's also much easier for them to sell the decision to hire Oniracom to their superiors or stakeholders. "They're the best at this," they'll say. "This is what they do."

Remember: in the end, the specialist is the safe choice. The specialist knows how to get it done because this is what they do. All things being equal (and remember, we can never allow anything to be equal!) the specialist will most often win the day. As long as your services are priced competitively, your niche will make you an attractive (and safe) choice for those looking to get it done right. And isn't that the kind of client and customer we are trying to attract?

Visibility COACH   The Visibility Coach says: Don't promote your vast array of services. Lead with one thing and proclaim your leadership in that niche.

The Most Important Person in the Room

Have you ever noticed how hard it is to dislike someone who really likes you? Even if others tend to dislike this person, you'll think: "He isn't so bad." Of course, none of this applies to stalkers and others who like you a little too much, but in general, people who like us tend to treat us well, give us their full attention, and we like them back.

Regardless of your politics, former President Bill Clinton had earned a reputation for truly focusing his attention on the person he was talking to, despite whoever else was around. People would comment that they felt like the most important person in the room when he spoke to them. But in this age of hyper-networking, cell phones, CrackBerrys, and the myriad of other distractions—getting the attention of anyone, let alone the person sitting across from you, is a challenge. The eye-darter, head-nodder, and general Uh-huh-er has become far too prevalent and acceptable in our culture.

This is not meant as simply a diatribe on the state of our interpersonal communication, but a recognition that an opportunity exists for those in business to capitalize on this dynamic to enhance their personal brand and reputation. When something is so conspicuous in its absence, or unexpectedly becomes present, it is recognized and remembered.

Maybe it's when your kids are all out with friends that it strikes you how quiet it is in your house. Maybe it's the evening sky, far from city lights, so filled with stars. Or it's the dinner date that actually asks you more questions about you than talks about themselves. Attention has become an endangered species and so is valued when given fully.

What's unfortunate is how seldom we actually recognize the behavior. Just as we don't normally verbalize and call attention to someone displaying undesirable public behavior (such as nose-picking), we do generally notice it and how it makes us feel.

Children, of course, have no qualms about pointing out these behaviors. My six-year-old son will physically take my face in his hands and turn my head in his direction to get my attention. And as all parents know well, nothing energizes our children more than when Mommy or Daddy gives them full attention and responds to every nuance as they tell us one of their wonderful stories.

But in crowded, social environments, it's far more difficult (and that much more appreciated) for us to turn off our surroundings and give someone our full attention.

A high school acting teacher of mine observed human behavior by noting how differently men and women hold a simple wine glass and drink from it. "Men," he explained, "look into their glass when they drink to see what's in the glass and how much is left. Women look over the top of the glass when they drink to see who is on the other side."

We are social creatures, so it can be a challenge to focus our eyes and attention on one person when others are around. But it can be a phenomenal skill to develop, and it takes a conscious effort to maintain it. The initial impact can be striking and the lasting benefits profound.

Personal and professional branding is about how you arrive, how you behave, and how you are remembered. Being liked can be the grease that helps personal relationships slide easily into business ones.

Do your prospects feel liked by you? Are you more worried about the business you might miss in a room, or are you appreciative of the potential business sitting across from you? Remember, a bird in the hand . . .

Visibility COACH   The Visibility Coach says: People like others who like them. Like them.

Get Over Yourself

"You are brilliant," I said to myself as I completed the first draft of the brochure for a new program I was launching. In fact, a client (and good friend) gave me a great idea— and I ran with it. I had the one-sheet brochure laid out, the text was expertly crafted, and the design was top-notch. I was ready to send it out to business prospects and could just envision the money rolling in.

Then I thought to myself: "Maybe I'll send it out to some colleagues and trusted advisors to get their take on it before it goes to the masses—just for the heck of it." I had expected a few responses pointing out some typos and perhaps an inadvertent fragmented sentence. What I got instead was a verbal beat-down, a veritable barrage of comments, criticisms, pointed suggestions, outright nay-sayers, and only a few (largely undeserved) pats on my back. Ouch!

The fact is that few of us do our best work alone; yet too many of us are relegated to create, strategize, and implement our ideas in isolation. And while I'm not suggesting that we float every idea and concept to everyone we know before we take action, our formal and informal colleagues and advisors can play a crucial role in ensuring that we produce quality work—before our clients and prospects receive it.

Remember that your professional brand is everything you do and everything that you fail to do well in your business. Everything that leaves your office—by phone, e-mail, snail mail, fax, printed, or otherwise—reflects on how your clients and prospects perceive you. Most organizations have horror stories of marketing pieces that were sent out with incorrect contact information, event dates, or other important information conspicuously absent.

In fact, I get dozens of calls every week from confused Canadians wishing to add more time on their Rogers Telecom prepaid phone cards. It seems that someone over at Rogers forgot to check to see if the phone number printed on the cards was correct. In fact, the number was perfect—*if* you wanted to reach the Visibility Coach in Castle Rock, Colorado. However, if you wanted to give money to Rogers for additional phone time, you are out of luck. A huge loss of revenue for them—and an ongoing pain in the neck for me!

I have spoken at numerous conferences and have served on many panels with journalists who always regale me with engaging, yet painful stories of press materials that contained poorly conceived wording or outright mistakes. I have never, ever heard of one of these cases where a positive story resulted from such an effort. Never.

While your advisory group can play a very important role in pointing out typographical errors and potential strategic land mines, or proposing alternative approaches to your marketing efforts, keep in mind that they can also fall victim to the focus group effect. This dynamic is illustrated by people's tendency to offer opinions because they think they're supposed to— whether they actually have strong feeling one way or another. The danger comes from making a serious about-face on a strategy based on one or two opinions from people not really qualified to offer them. If it makes sense to you, then go with it. Always take external factors and feedback into consideration; but in general, look for trends and follow your well-informed gut.

(Special note: If you do have access to educated friends or strong industry contacts, respect their time. Turn to your advisors, but don't go to the well too often. Either pay for their expertise, return the favor, or throw some business their way. Hey, we all work for a living!)

As for my program, I was grateful for all the responses I received. Some suggestions I followed, while others didn't quite fit my vision. All the feedback was tremendously valuable. In the end, the questions were answered, the benefits clarified, the audience narrowed, and the materials significantly revised.

In short, we can easily become enamored with our own brilliant ideas. It often takes a light shining from a different direction to illuminate the flaws in our approach. Turn those lights on and keep your eyes and ears open to alternatives.

___

Visibility COACH   The Visibility Coach says: Keep telling yourself that you're brilliant; but also make sure that nothing leaves your office that hasn't been reviewed and doesn't live up to that standard. Your brand depends on it.

___

Your Name Sucks

Like death and taxes, if you are in business someone will inevitably utter an expletive connected to you or your company's name. It's a given. It could come from a dissatisfied client, or even an unfriendly competitor. And depending on where they say it, and to whom, it could be very, very dangerous for your business.

Despite our best efforts, we know that we can't satisfy every client or customer every time; eventually someone will be less than thrilled with the results of your business relationship (or from the threat you pose as a competitor). As they say, reputation rules, and a motivated, dissatisfied individual or group can wreak havoc with your reputation and even destroy your livelihood. And if you think that a Draconian scenario like this is unlikely and doesn't apply to you—wake up!

A generation ago, we used talk about "the general public"; you know, the average Joe or Jane on the street. Well, guess what? They don't exist anymore. Now, instead of the general public, we have a variety of publics that we must address, communicate with, cater to, contend with, and be cautious of.

In yesteryear, an unsatisfied customer might be motivated to write a letter to the editor, complain to the Better Business Bureau, or maybe even grab a picket sign and set up camp in front of your office. Today's unhappy camper is altogether different—and potentially far more damaging to your reputation and livelihood.

The Internet has given a voice to the downtrodden and the disgruntled; the inconvenienced and the inconsolable; the fed-up and furious. A 55-year-old man with a beef about anything from a barking dog to a late-arriving package used to be relegated to sitting in his robe at 1:00 in the morning complaining to his wife. Today, that same person spends half the night furiously typing on a keyboard and ranting to the masses. And if you think that no one is listening—you are *so* twentieth century.

While the rest of us are fast asleep—dreaming of compelling new marketing campaigns, successful go-to-market strategies, and exciting new product launches—search engines are working away, finding every mention of your name, every reference to your company—without regard to truth, your business objectives, or anyone's motivations.

As we awake to face the new day, countless prospects are logging-on to computers around the world and searching for products, services, experts, and resources. Unfortunately, they are learning more than simply what you want them to know about your business; they are learning what others want them to know and think about you and your business as well.

The doomsday scenario: Despite your best efforts and quality service, a client has unrealistic expectations and is unhappy about the results of your business exchange. You try to work out a reasonable compromise, but he is having none of it. He is loaded for bear and he wants satisfaction. Translation: He wants revenge.

So he goes online and registers the domain name: "The Name of Your Company Sucks.com." He then proceeds to create a basic web site and a blog and begins to rant about his dispute with you. Moreover, he posts profanity-laced tirades on a daily basis and encourages others to do the same. Before long, his rants are being referenced on other people's blogs and the critical mass of name mentions achieves the unthinkable: It gains a high ranking on the search engines. In fact, it beats the ranking of your official site and appears higher on the search page than you do! Your prospective clients begin learning about you first—not from your official web site—but from someone who wants to defame you.

An unlikely scenario? *Au contraire!* It has happened time and time again to some very well known companies, and to some lesser known ones as well. The saboteurs have come from the ranks of customers, competitors, neighbors, employees—and even family members. Some organizations had the resources to weather the storm, while others were crushed under the weight of the bad visibility. The real tragedy is that there is very little you can do about it once it occurs. It can take years—even decades—to build a positive reputation and only a matter of days to destroy it.

Because you can never ensure that everyone will be happy with you and your business, the least you can—and must—do is remove the easy online weapons that might be used to assault you and your business's reputation. Speaker and leading guru on search engine optimization (SEO) and Pay-Per-Click (PPC) marketing and author of *The Findability Formula*, Heather Lutze, suggests that—as uncomfortable as it might seem—you register and own the domain names: "(yourbusinessname)sucks.com" as well as every variation of your business name, including adding the word "the" (as in, theCocaColaCompany.) Beyond that, you should register the dreaded "F" word before your name as well. You'd be astonished at how many malcontents resort to creating web pages called "F"Company X.com in an effort to exact revenge.

Trust me, it will be disturbing viewing those domain names on the screen as you are purchasing them; but take comfort in the fact that you own them and no one else does—or can. Then just keep the names parked with no web site, and never let them expire. If a name never gets posted, it'll never be found on the search engines.

The takeaway: Guard your name. Guard your brand. Guard your reputation. Beyond the importance of providing good work and good service to your clients, take proactive steps to ensure that your visibility online is the result of your hard efforts—and not in spite of them. Sometimes the greatest visibility strategy is knowing when it's best to remain invisible.

Visibility COACH   The Visibility Coach says: Don't let anybody else own your name—in any form.

Forever . . . and Ever

I was standing by the dugout, hanging on the fence and chatting with the father of one of the girls on my oldest daughter's softball team. As he and I chatted about the challenges of raising kids—in particular, our frequent struggles with the brooding nature of teenage girls—he said something that really struck me.

"I always have to remember, especially with my girls," he told me, "that everything I say to them is being recorded." Profound! The words we say to our children are important, since those words help to paint the picture in their mind of who they are and who they will be in the future. It is the same with our personal and professional brand.

In the age of the Internet and digital information, virtually nothing is ever lost, deleted, or truly disposed of. The inappropriate photos of you and your college friends in various stages of inebriation, the late-night politically charged diatribe posted on your blog, the inappropriate joke that you e-mailed to your best friend with explicit instructions "not to forward to anyone!"—all of these things still exist somewhere, and likely will for the duration of your life and beyond.

Tattoos were once thought to be permanent. Now, they can largely be removed by special lasers. Your vasectomy can be reversed, death penalties can be commuted, and lifetime bans from sports rarely are. But the Internet? That, my friends, is forever. And while I understand the temptation to wave-off or dismiss this admonition—as you rationalize that you are not likely to be a girl that will ever go wild again, that your drunken teen days are behind you, and you've never ranted online in your jammies at 3:00 A.M.—don't be too quick to assume that you are immune from future skeletons being exposed. And remember: This is all about crafting, maintaining, protecting, and promoting your brand.

In addition to the things you say, post, forward, upload and download, the things you do and say in public are also susceptible to online immortality. Most cell phones these days record not only pictures, but video as well. And while there are always some very clever and professionally produced videos posted online with the likes of YouTube and other online sharing sites, some of the best video are the scenes and scenarios that are caught or captured by others. Those embarrassing moments may languish in obscurity or spread like wildfire. Either way, they are out there—way out there.

You would also be wrong to assume that most potentially damaging information or images would emanate from you. Other people are perfectly capable of posting pictures, false accusations, or mentioning you in an online diatribe about . . . anything. Anyone can criticize you or your business online and influence others' perceptions of you. Their words will last as well.

While there are basic things you can do to keep your image safe and clean, in general, effective brand management requires a diligent effort to seek out and discover images, mentions, and information about you and your business on a daily basis. Fortunately, much of the effort can be automated through Google News Alerts and other services.

Another great service is Pipl.com. Pipl uses a different algorithm to conduct a broad online search for mentions of your name, or anyone else you want to search. Are you ready for a potentially nerve-racking exercise? Do a Pipl.com search of your children's names—especially if you have teenagers. I was ready to hurt the kid who mentioned my daughter's name in his blog rant, until I realized that he actually said something complimentary. Whew!

The point is that it is indeed a different world. We have to be far more careful about what we say, write, or release online or in public. Just as when we take our wedding vows and promise to stay together "till death do us part," even death won't likely impact the digital vows that we take every time we hit the "send" button.

Visibility COACH The Visibility Coach says: In the Disney classic *Bambi*, Thumper's Mom was right. "If you can't say somethin' nice . . . "

Guard Your Good Name

"I've got to show you this," my buddy says as he pulls a magazine out of his briefcase during a casual lunch meeting. He throws a large trade publication on the table, flips it over to the back cover, and slides it toward me. I see a beautiful, full-color, back-page ad from Pepsi thanking Kahala, one of the fastest-growing franchise operators in America with such popular brands as Cold Stone Creamery, Blimpie Subs, Cereality, and several other restaurants. Clearly, Kahala is an important customer to Pepsi.

"What am I looking for?" I ask my friend.

"Just read it again!" he urges with a big smile on his face.

As I continue to study the ad, the source of his bemusement becomes immediately apparent. The headline read: ***"Thank you, Kahala, for your continued support."***

Wow. With only six words on the whole page (not counting the client's actual name) that comes to an almost 17 percent typo rate! Yikes! Somebody's gonna get a butt whoppin' over this!

The obvious admonition is that you need to proofread your copy before going to print; that's the no-brainer. Bad typos are what kept Jay Leno's audiences howling on during the "headlines" segments on the *Tonight Show*. No, the point is that you can never allow or expect others to guard your reputation. Every time your name, your logo, voice, or signature is used, it must come ultimately from you, or at the very least, yours must be the final eyes that review the outgoing communication before it is launched into the world.

Of course, we all know that mistakes happen. People are generally forgiving and lighthearted about oversights and typos, and they rarely result in anything approaching disaster for your company. But I say—it shouldn't matter. It's been allowed to happen. Just as a dirty bathroom at a local eatery makes everything else in the establishment suspect, poor oversight with your marketing messages only serves to diminish your reputation and credibility in the marketplace. "If they don't proofread their own stuff, what will they do with mine?"

The truth is that there is just no excuse for it. There is always someone available to provide a quick once-over and others, outside your business, should never be allowed to both create *and* approve a message with your name attached to it. *Never*.

While the U.S. President has speechwriters, he always reviews and edits the words that will be attributed to him. Advertising agencies can create marketing pieces, television commercials, and electronic newsletters, but someone from your organization has to review, edit, and approve them. You also have to be obsessive about protecting your graphic standards and logo usage. Just because someone is holding a charity event benefiting your organization, that doesn't mean they get to use your logo any way they wish. You must approve such usage first!

I handled the news media for The Children's Hospital in Denver in the early 1990s. One day, I got a call from a reporter that a female member of the state legislature was calling a press conference to claim that Children's Hospital had held a charity golf tournament over the weekend and hired strippers to perform. Needless to say, I scrambled to learn the facts of the situation. Finally, I found out that a nightclub owner had decided to make The Children's Hospital the beneficiary of his annual charity golf tournament and had some of his scantily-clad "girls" staff the holes and pose for pictures with the competitors.

The tournament used The Children's Hospital logo and featured the name prominently in both the promotional material and at the event itself. What was *not* clear, however, was the fact that the hospital had nothing to do with the event. We didn't help conceive, plan, promote, or implement it; we were merely to be the beneficiary of the proceeds. In the end, fearing the negative press, our CEO publicly distanced himself from the event and returned all the donations. Unfortunate. Our Foundation—the fundraising arm of the hospital—should have had their tentacles out and intervened earlier to ensure that no hanky-panky would be connected with the hospital's name and reputation.

In the Pepsi ad fiasco, the person who created the ad likely was made the heavy in the situation; but I assert that the marketing person at Pepsi, who did more than simply delegate the responsibility, but actually abdicated it, should bear the brunt of the sanctions. For a multi-gazzillion-dollar brand's good name to be attached to such an easily averted blunder is inexcusable. The positive result for the rest of us is that it has served as an unintentional case study of how *not* to protect your brand, your public image, and good name.

The takeaway: Have clear policies and procedures for how materials are reviewed prior to dissemination. Develop specific graphic standards for how and when your logo or name can be used and how approval is sought and granted, and make the consequences for violating the policy unusually harsh.

Visibility COACH   The Visibility Coach says: There is no lost and found that you can visit to get your reputation back. Don't let go of it.

Connecting Flights

In not very long ago yesteryear, travel was exciting—even glamorous at times. Ahh, to see new places around the world, to jet-off to distant cities . . . but that was then. Today, it's hard to go anywhere. Not that it's not interesting to be in new places; it's just the getting there and coming back that sucks.

"So where ya headed?" 13B says to my 13A.

"Oh God, please don't be a talker," I think to myself. "Just go to sleep and try not to drool on my shoulder." "Uh, just heading to Dallas—for business," I add hastily, answering the inevitable next question.

I admit it. I've become the "distant traveler"—the guy that gives short answers and puts the headphones on. By and large, on a domestic flight, I just want to be left alone. What happened to me? I used to love to chat up the guy or gal in the next seat. I'd learn about their work and we'd find some common issues with our kids.

I guess it's just the volume of travel, the number of times I've taken my shoes off and done the "perp-walk" through the metal detector in recent years. I'm tired of trying to shoehorn my 6′4″ frame into an economy seat next to the big fat guy. (Apologies to big fat guys everywhere.)

Today, more and more travelers talk less and less. For us frequent business travelers, there is a secret fraternity. A common demeanor that says: "I don't really want to be here and would prefer to be left alone to endure this leg of my travel."

But I've learned that it doesn't always pay to be that guy. There are times when it's reasonable to adopt the "don't talk to me" posture, but there are other times when you want to connect with your seatmate, and it often has to do with your, and their, attire.

For years, I always opted for comfort when traveling, often wearing jeans and a polo shirt or even occasionally donning a cool superhero t-shirt. As I arrived in Philadelphia a few years ago to do some work with a colleague, I was dressed very casually, having packed my nicer clothes for the next day's meetings.

Hall-of-Fame speaker and workplace professionalism guru Marjorie Brody pulled up to the curb at passenger pick-up and greeted me with a hug. As I climbed into the passenger seat, she began to put the car in gear but instead stopped, turned, and looked me up and down. "Don't ever get on a plane looking like that again," she scolded me.

"What do you mean?" I laughed dismissively. "We're friends," I asserted. "I don't need to impress you."

"I'm not joking," she continued. "This isn't just about dressing for success and presenting yourself well—which you should be doing more often. It's about missed opportunities to meet and connect with other professionals. You will never know about the business you didn't get today, the introduction that will not be forthcoming, and the potential partner who will not wish to explore collaboration—because they never met you! You were not a professional during your travel, so you were never noticed by other professionals."

She was right. If I had a tail, it would now be planted firmly between my legs. Why would someone be interested in me and my business when they would never have a reason to believe that I actually ran a business? I might have invited a comment or conversation about my Underdog® t-shirt, but it's not likely the kind of conversation I would have welcomed.

In the days since, as I began to travel to more speaking engagements, a remarkable thing started happening: I connected with the right people—more and more. Whether at an airport or in flight, I've begun to recognize an interesting dynamic among business travelers. It's sort of an unwritten understanding that says: "I want to be left alone, but if you look successful, I am open to a (brief) interaction." It starts with an offhand comment about the bout of turbulence, an "excuse me" as we reach for the overhead compartment, or a "sorry" as we inadvertently kick their leg while adjusting our seat.

"Business?" you might say simply. "Yea, just heading home. Pretty quick in and out," they respond. If they then put on their Bose noise-canceling headphones, you know the interaction is complete. But if they offer up a: "How 'bout you?"

the dance has begun. Only you can decide to sit it out, or dance.

I'm not going to launch into a primer on networking and inter-personal communications. The point is that most successful people have to endure some travel as an essential element of their work. When you figure in the cost of the plane ticket and hotel, the odds are strong that a reasonable percentage of the people on your flight are involved in a successful business as well. That concentration of professionals creates opportunities. Of course, the closer you are to the front section of the plane the better your chances.

Something very interesting and tangible happens when I travel "business class," regardless of where I am sitting on the plane: People are curious about me and often I am open to connecting with them. I've compiled a valuable stack of business cards and a few great clients directly resulting from a chance meeting during travel–when I am dressed well.

How you arrive—or embark, in this instance—can play a significant role in who you meet and the interaction that occurs. Dressing like a professional when in the presence of, and in proximity to other professionals greatly influences their perception of you and the subsequent conversation that ensues. I have met prospects when casually dressed who were interested in what I did, but as my profession clearly did not match my persona, I never heard from these people again.

Visibility COACH The Visibility Coach says: When you travel, or are out among professionals, don't dress for comfort—dress for business.

Turn That $#+!* Down!

So, I'm sitting in a back booth at Panera Bread, getting a little work done between meetings on the road, but struggling to concentrate. It's not that the ideas aren't flowing; it's that there is a guy about 20 feet away talking so loudly about his investment strategies and philosophy and throwing F-bombs around like they were candy, that I am going out of my mind! But you know what? Public profanity is not candy—it's poison.

It is likely that this bozo actually believes what he has to say is so important that everyone would rather listen to his diatribes and watch his flailing arm gestures than enjoy their meal with their companions.

"No, it's okay, buddy. You just keep talking. Sorry—was my chewing bothering you? Yes, I think that woman in the red blouse is inconsiderate to be trying to talk with her 4-year-old son about his T-ball game. No, you go ahead. Clearly, what you have to say is more important. Oh, and it's probably good that all these kids are hearing those bad words today. They'll learn them eventually anyway, right?"

Sorry, did I say that out loud? No, but I should have. The moms have packed up their kids and moved around to the far side of the restaurant, but I'm going to sit here and keep writing to present a graphic example of the importance of how you arrive. Chances are that this creep has no idea how he is being perceived by those around him. Something in his past has led him to believe that this approach is effective. Maybe his strategy is akin to the old E.F Hutton ads, where when E.F. Hutton talks, people listen. Yes, but—the voice is grating and the words repel.

Why am I so worked up about this? I guess there is just something about his approach that sets me off. This is true for all of us in some respect. There are television commercials, product jingles, and media personalities that rub us the wrong way as well. They've likely achieved a measure of success, but I wonder, at what cost?

You can, of course, adopt the attitude that you can't please everyone. But how much potential business are you losing by repelling some percentage of your prospects? I'm not suggesting you water down your message or approach to make it appeal to the masses; I'm saying that it doesn't have to be either/or. You can be wildly creative, out-of-the box in your approach, and even flashy in your style, without alienating prospects.

Rush Limbaugh has made a nice career from his in-your-face, over-the-top ranting to the Republican faithful (I'm not taking sides here. Just reporting the facts, ma'am). It has worked so well for Rush because he knows his audience—and that's his only audience. He doesn't need to please or impress the other side. But how many of us have such a well-defined and polarized market that we can afford to offend anyone?

Do you really take time to step back or be introspective? Do you strategically consider what you say, who you say it to, and how you come across? Do you think that people who can't handle cursing in a public place need to lighten up? All right, you may not be the loudmouth at the table by the window refusing to take a breath between boasting; but are you completely free of guilt?

Only you can decide whether you have anything to work on in terms of your professional behavior. The point is that you must take the time to examine and ask the question:

How am I being perceived—not just by my associates but by those in proximity? Are you taking control of your brand and how you are seen, heard, thought of, regarded, and remembered, or are you blissfully unaware of your impact? I'm just asking.

Alright, I'm dead serious here: this blowhard just walked over to me on his way out and said: "I saw you looking over here a lot and I thought you must be very interested in what I was talking about. Give me a call if you have an interest in my venture!" And then he slapped his business card down on the table in front of me.

"No, Buddy," I replied politely. "You were just very loud and I was struggling to concentrate on my work." "Whatever," he responds. "Call me if you are interested."

With his address in hand, I think I'll just send him a copy of this book—and flag this page!

Visibility COACH   The Visibility Coach says: Most in business have an unwritten "No jerks" rule. Don't be one.

Jump On It

It can take years, even decades to build a great reputation and only a moment to destroy it, perhaps forever.

"He was always such a nice man and a quiet neighbor," they would say of the accused axe-murderer. But it doesn't take a crime to cast doubt on your credibility, capabilities, and quality. And doubt is deadly to your brand. While many in business will face some level of crisis (however you define one), how well you handle that challenge and how fast it is resolved can often mean the difference between success and failure.

It took well over a decade for Exxon to overcome the memory of the 1989 Valdez oil spill; and I'm not sure that Mel Gibson will ever fully regain his Hollywood goodwill after his much-publicized, alcohol-fueled, anti-Semitic rant. And wasn't O.J. Simpson best known for his football accomplishments at one point?

In most cases, it is unreasonable to expect that a good PR response can transform a bad situation into a good one. Often the best outcome is to simply mitigate the potential damage and move on in a depleted state.

Celebrities, with a proper (and immediate) mea culpa, can often recover their image following a drunk driving arrest, or a prostitution solicitation, but if they were belligerent, caused injury, or took lives during the act, or if it was a repeat offense, recovery can be far more challenging. Some incidents are so profound that the very nature of the offense is contrary to the core brand. These situations are virtually unrecoverable, and the best that can be hoped for is to avoid a lengthy prison stay.

But the keys to recovery for most scenarios are simply expediency and transparency. Tell the truth, and tell it quickly. Any delay only ensures that people will talk about the event longer and that the images will become more firmly ingrained in their minds. Bad stories, quickly resolved, can be overcome. Bad stories, dragged out, can be devastating for your business.

Of course, the exception to the admonition is when there are pressing legal implications, but those circumstances are not the norm. In the lion's share of instances, the truth of what has transpired will ultimately come to light. Better to deal with it quickly, acknowledge what occurred, and move on.

Some years back, I worked with a very popular Colorado pizza chain that is well known with local residents and visiting skiers from around the world. Known for its rustic interior and creative "Mountain Pies," Beau Jo's Pizza had ten locations and has been a local favorite for over 30 years. I got a call one morning from the company's president, who told me that the local radio station's high-profile consumer watchdog reporter was on the line, and that a customer had told the station that bugs were crawling around one of their restaurants. The reporter wanted someone to go on the radio show and face the accusations.

"What should we do?" my client asked, clearly concerned.

"Well, is it true?" I asked.

After discovering that indeed it was—although isolated to one location—I told him to ask the reporter if we could have 30 minutes to get all the facts for him, and that we would gladly come on his radio show and discuss the matter. The host agreed, and we went to work.

A mere thirty minutes later, I went on-air as the company's representative and the exchange went something like this:

Radio host (exasperated): "So Dolores is sitting and eating her pizza and a bug crawls across her foot. She looks down and sees bugs everywhere! We have David Avrin on the line. Dave—what is going on here?!"

Me: "Well Tom, first I need to tell you that this is absolutely true. It is an interesting set of circumstances that we'll likely laugh about years from now, but we are not laughing now. The fact is that we work hard to replicate the rustic feel of our original mountain location in all our restaurants, but apparently, along with the split pine logs that decorate our walls, have come some unwelcome guests—pine beetles! At our Buckingham location only, where we recently remodeled, the logs were apparently not sealed properly and the beetles that lived within them have hatched.

"So here's what we've done. We have closed that location immediately. As we speak, we are stripping the logs off the walls and removing all the wood from the building. We have pest control coming in this afternoon with safe and effective compounds that will clear the entire restaurant of any insects; a large, doubled-staff cleaning crew is coming in to work throughout the night; and health inspectors are scheduled for tomorrow morning to ensure that the restaurant is clean and safe for our guests. Our plan is to reopen tomorrow for lunch, in what I promise will be the ugliest restaurant you have ever seen, but with the same great pizza you have come to love over the past 30 years. All other restaurants have been checked and none has the same issue."

"As for the woman who brought this to our attention, she gets free pizza for a year."

The radio host spent the next ten minutes talking about how much he loved Beau Jo's pizza and how he likes to dip the crust in honey. What else could he say at that point? What could he say the next day? It was done. The problem was solved. There was nothing to ask, nothing to investigate or reveal.

But what if the question of health, safety, and cleanliness at this restaurant chain had been allowed to fester for even a day or two? It would likely have meant the end of the line for Beau Jo's. Today, they flourish.

Only so much can be done to prevent challenges to your business and your reputation. But in responding quickly—not just with words, but with actions intended to actually *solve the problem*—you can often eliminate the story altogether and move on.

Visibility COACH   The Visibility Coach says: Address problems quickly, honestly, and effectively. Every minute you delay, doubles the amount of time the problem will remain an issue.

Who "Nose" You?

I saw a video clip the other day of a junior high kid from the 1970s with his face buried in a piece of copy paper, fresh from the mimeograph machine. I realize that this visual has no significance for people born after 1980, but for the rest of us, a big smile is likely on your face. Or better yet, a big smile on your nose!

Think about some of the great smells in your life. I'm not simply referring to a big steak on the grill, a dozen roses, or fresh bread baking. I'm talking about the smells that have become part of a marketplace experience, the kind of smells that could be identified (by brand name) in a blindfold test—the unmistakable scent of an open container of Play-Doh, the fruity goodness of a pack of Juicy Fruit gum, and the enticing aroma of Chanel #5.

Our brains connect smells to memories, and our memories to feelings and emotions. Who among us hasn't experienced an eerie flashback and long-forgotten memories triggered by a familiar smell? Maybe it's chocolate chip cookies coming out of the oven at your grandmother's house, or when you bump into someone wearing the unmistakable scent that was worn by an old flame. It's powerful; that much is for sure.

Here's an odd question: How do *you* smell, and does it really matter? I know that I've been drawn to a tradeshow booth simply by the smell of a popcorn machine. Cheap ploy? Sure, but it worked! Is your establishment filled with the aroma of coffee, burgers, or other scents enjoyed by your customers? Is your retail location's bathroom odor replacing your value proposition as the chief takeaway with your customers?

You may think that the subject of smell is a bit out-of-place in a book about marketing and branding, but tell that to the people at Starbucks, Regal Cinemas, Procter and Gamble, or Oscar Meyer.

Okay, this may not apply to you and your business, but then again, it might. Being visible and being remembered and known (in the way you want to be) requires a careful examination of *all* your touch points. Is there an opportunity to touch your customers aromatically? Do you smell great, or at least clean? Does your business smell great? Is this an opportunity you are overlooking? I'm just asking.

Visibility COACH   The Visibility Coach says: Your customer's nose matters. Don't blow it.

Zoned-Out

A faint and very groggy voice came to me on the phone. "Uh . . . yah . . . hello?"

"James?" I asked sheepishly. "Sorry, did I wake you?"

"Yes," the groggy voice said, "It's 5:00 A.M. but it's okay. Don't worry about it. I need to get up anyway. What can I do for you?" he asks, trying to be polite.

I'm sitting in my New York hotel at about 8:00 A.M., and didn't even consider the time difference on the west coast. Have you ever done that? And then you try to apologize and tell the person you've waked up to go back to bed, but of course they can't. Either way, you just keep thinking about what an idiot you are. Unfortunately, you're not the only one thinking this.

Now, this might seem like a basic issue, but in an increasingly global marketplace, time-zone issues are growing in importance. For instance, one of my favorite graphic designers,* and a good friend, is located in Sri Lanka—a 14-hour time difference! We talk about projects real-time over Skype, and I need to know what time it is for him. I also have clients in Singapore, Bangkok, and London; web-development providers in Pakistan and India; a PowerPoint guru in the United Arab Emirates; and the pages of my media training guide were designed by a great guy in central Russia.

Your marketing and promotional efforts can be impacted by time zone issues close to home as well. If a reporter or producer for a national news network in New York or Atlanta has a 3:00 P.M. deadline for a story that will provide tremendous exposure for your business, it's important for you to have your ducks in a row and to recognize that her 3:00 P.M. deadline is actually 1:00 P.M. or 2:00 P.M. or even noon for the rest of the United States. Screw that up, and you're screwed.

If you are sending out a promotional press release shortly after you get to work at around 8:30 A.M. your time in Los

Angeles, just know that most of the stories being considered by the national media outlets on the east coast have already been decided for the day—likely hours ago. Your customers, clients, prospects, partners, suppliers, and others are all doing different things at any point in the day—much of it depending on what time it is where they are.

If you are making sales calls, prospecting inquiries and media pitches, be cognizant of work start times, meal times, and media deadlines throughout the country. You don't want to finally make that connection with a hard-to-reach prospect on his cell phone only to be told that he is tied up in a lunch meeting and will have to get back to you.

Is this important? Only in measuring how important first impressions are. Do you want to be known, remembered, and potentially defined by your careless outreach during an inappropriate or inopportune time, or by your savvy and strategic communication endeavors?

Visibility COACH   The Visibility Coach says: Watch your watch.

*Shameless plug: Mohammed Sadath—Hometown Creative Design, Sri Lanka *hometowncd@yahoo.com*

You Clean Up Real Nice (Dress for Success: Part Two)

Do you know someone that always looks impeccable? You know, the colleague or customer that just knows how to dress and make a good impression. What is it about these people that makes them memorable?

Then there are those with their own signature look. It could be hairstylist Jose Ebert with his trademark little cowboy hat, or Steve Jobs with his intentionally hip and casual black t-shirt and jeans.

The truth is that the whole concept of dressing for success means different things to different people and you need to tailor your visual message to your audience, just as you tailor your verbal and written messages.

This is not meant as a primer on color choices or the need to sit up straight and look your prospects in the eye; that's too basic. This admonition is simple recognition of the fact that you can gain a strategic advantage in a competitive marketplace by taking the time to be strategic and intentional about how you arrive, how you are perceived and ultimately remembered.

Remember that everything you do and don't do during a business pitch or transaction is observed, evaluated, scrutinized, and ultimately will influence the decision of the buyer.

Just ask the retail industry if a product's package matters, and ask the fashion industry if attractive models are important. Poll the automakers and inquire how critical color choice is to their buyers. Why, then, would you think it would be any different when we are trying to sell ourselves as the chief brand ambassadors for our companies?

A professional stylist can certainly be of value, but most of us, with some careful consideration, can make smart choices about how we are perceived in our business relationships and the messages we want to send. Just as a tired and outdated medical office can lead prospective clients to question how up to date, or state of the art, a cosmetic surgery center might be, so too does your appearance send an important message about your level of knowledge and perceived level of success.

Why do you think that realtors place such importance on their dress and the kind of car they drive? They know that if they look very successful, clients will think that they must be really good at their job and they'll be more likely to hire them to list their home. And it's true. Your house is likely the biggest purchase you will ever make. You need confidence that your realtor isn't going to screw it up. The ones that drive a really expensive car look like they're doing well. Translation: less risky. For them, arriving as "successful" becomes a self-fulfilling prophecy.

Are you still living large, sporting a haircut that you've had for 20 years, but that really works well with your face? Or can't seem to give up your favorite super-comfy sweater, or still have tint to your glasses? It's time for an upgrade.

An important question to always keep in mind is: Do you dress for your industry, or for the customers you meet with? Financial industry professionals are well known for their buttoned-up, conservative attire, but if you take the same industry knowledge and make a presentation to ranchers in a rural community, you had best not be showin' up in them city-slicker duds.

Even if you spend most of your working hours slaving away in your sweats in a home office, you had better clean up well for your meetings away from the office.

Visibility COACH   The Visibility Coach says: How you dress, and who you dress for matters. (Everything matters.)

Bring in the Closer

It's the bottom of the ninth inning, two men on base, one out, and the starting pitcher has been struggling. The manager calls *"Time"* and begins a slow walk toward the pitcher's mound while motioning to the bullpen. The closer grabs his glove and jogs toward the mound.

It's amazing how often sports mirrors business. Perhaps it's the competitive nature of both or that generally two sides are involved in a transaction. You'll hear a plethora of sports analogies in the business world, such as: making a pitch, getting up to bat, in the home-stretch, nearing the finish line, the end-zone, hitting a presentation out of the park, or hitting a competitor when they're down.

I would submit that the most crucial sports-related dynamic in business is recognizing the importance of the closer. In reality, the prospect of a business transaction being successful is not possible without the completion of the transaction. From money being exchanged across a retail counter, to a handshake following labor negotiations, or the mind-numbing plethora of documents being signed to complete a real estate purchase—the deal has to be completed or it's not really a deal.

The question that you need to ask—and occasionally re-evaluate—is: Who is the best person to make that happen? While your marketing messages may be delivered by actors, jingles, or other promotional images, the organization's leader is often carrying the banner for the brand. And while often the company leader is the ideal representative to serve as the face of the organization and chief brand ambassador, they (you) may not be the best one to get the deals done.

When it comes to closing sales, things can get a bit tricky. Skills can vary wildly, and the skills and expertise necessary to peruse a balance sheet, secure funding, or develop new technologies, aren't likely the same skills needed to sell them. Some straddle the line fairly well, others merely get in the way.

A famous exchange in the movie *Schindler's List* between Ben Kingsley and Liam Neeson illustrated the sometimes murky waters of leadership roles.

> *Itzhak Stern: Let me understand. They put up all the money. I do all the work. What, if you don't mind my asking, would you do?*
>
> *Oskar Schindler: I'd make sure it's known the company's in business. I'd see that it had a certain . . . panache. That's what I'm good at. Not the work, not the work . . . the presentation.*

When you consider your image, your brand, and how you as a business professional or owner are known, you must honestly ask yourself what your visible role should be. You have to be honest with yourself about whether you help or hinder the completion of the final transactions.

I know some very astute business leaders who understand that they must get out of the way of their trained sales professionals and let them do what they were hired to do. Many of them also work very closely with their sales staff and show up at the most crucial part of the process to lend additional "gravitas," or weight and credibility, to the negotiations. They know that, just as a car salesperson will often play the game of going into the back room to get "approval" from his superiors, so too can bringing in the top leader to the final stages give a sense to the prospect that the business relationship is so important to the company that the leader him-or herself felt it was worth their time. This can be very powerful.

Conversely, if a company leader lacks the interpersonal skill set or financial know-how to truly communicate the capabilities and features of their offering—then a colleague should be empowered to represent the value proposition and ask for the sale. If you are the company's leader, only you can determine where you fall on the spectrum, but I would caution that you must bring others into the conversation to see if consensus is present.

As you work to craft, refine, and promote who you are in the marketplace, be careful to avoid assumptions and assigning roles based on hierarchy rather than talents. The key to successful marketing and delivering on the promise is to ensure that your actions mirror your message and that your brand ambassadors are the best suited for the job.

Visibility COACH   The Visibility Coach says: When you send a pinch-hitter up to bat at the end of the game, be sure that you've got the right hitter in the box (or the right closer on the mound).

The Path to Visibility:
Part 2 – Creating Awareness

Creating Awareness

Be Different
Be Assertive
Be Seen

The Fine Line

While watching TV recently, my 15-year-old daughter turned to me and asked a simple but profound question: "Dad," she said: "How do you become famous?"

Not recognizing the genesis of her question, my initial inclination was to dismiss her inquiry with a simple response along the lines of "Just get as many people as possible to know who you are." Or, I could have launched into an in-depth explanation of how I help my clients differentiate themselves, build their brand, and generate news media coverage for their businesses. But she would have glossed-over.

So instead, I paused, looked up from my magazine, glanced over at the MTV Video Music Awards she was watching on television, and realized that her perspective on fame was vastly different than that of my generation's.

In earlier times, fame was achieved when significant accomplishment met widespread public recognition. In the best of all worlds, those achievements were ones that others aspired to, such as creating a new invention, starring in a major motion picture, hitting a game-winning home run, mastering a musical instrument, performing a heroic feat, or setting a world record. Regrettably, many people have also achieved notoriety by committing heinous deeds, embarrassing acts, or becoming profound failures in a far too public way.

Today, the lines between fame and infamy are blurred. The heroes of today are often athletes, musicians, or movie stars who behave outrageously, disrespectfully, or even criminally. Consider O.J. Simpson, Paris Hilton, Eliot Spitzer, Lindsay Lohan, Heidi Fliess, or former Illinois Governor Rod Blagojevich. It's hard to argue their fame, but have they gained recognition for true accomplishment; or are they merely famous for their outrageous behavior?

Today, almost anyone can achieve a measure of fame by appearing on a reality show, game show, or even by posting a provocative video on YouTube. With the massive growth of 24-hour-a-day news media, including major network news, cable broadcasts, daily newspapers, countless trade publications, and online, up-to-the-minute news content, the hunger for good stories seems to be insatiable.

So, while many people wish to be famous for their business or personal achievements, industry wisdom, or political insights, these question must be asked: What does it take to *truly* achieve fame; what can it do for your business; and what does it look like when you get there?

I spoke to a large audience of business owners recently and asked: "By a show of hands, how many of you would like to be on the news tonight?" As you might expect, most hands were raised high in the air. I went on to instruct the audience on exactly how to make that happen: "First, you need to drive downtown, remove all your clothing, and hang from an overpass by a bungee cord. I guarantee," I said, "you'll make the evening news." But to what end?

Being famous by today's standards is easy enough in this day and age. The challenge is to be known in a way that is beneficial to your business and your reputation. You want to be famous for your expertise as the leader of your own category, and known by the people in your target market. Isn't it better to be known for excellence, expertise, and exclusivity—than, as the owner of the place where the fire or shooting took place? Achieving a level of fame will often help your business; infamy rarely will.

When the names of famous business leaders are mentioned, what thoughts come to mind? Where does their personal and professional brand register with you? I guess it depends on whose name is offered. Jack Welch gets a different response than Bernie Madoff. Walt Disney will likely trump Donald Trump, and Tom Brokaw ranks higher than Geraldo Rivera. More importantly, what thoughts are generated in the marketplace at the mention of your name?

A biblical quote offers: "A good name is more desirable than great riches; to be esteemed is better than silver or gold." I say the good name and the riches are often connected. Why? Because people want to do business with people whom they like and trust. They want to work with people who are great at what they do and who are easy to work with. A good reputation is essential for long-term business success.

In today's business world, fame can come simply by achieving broad awareness of your business—irrespective of the context. But your reputation equals your brand. A good, well-publicized brand is the prerequisite for true success. And while we have no direct control over our brand as it resides in the minds of our customers, prospects, and other audiences, we do have great influence over the future of the brand itself. Everything matters. It's what you say and what you are wise enough not to say. It's the class and credibility with which you promote yourself. It's the activities in which you choose to engage and what that says to whoever is listening.

Work toward achieving fame by crafting and promoting the personal brand you *want* the world to see. There are few actions or words that we can take back, and do-overs are rare. Take the wheel and keep steering in the right direction

So to my daughter, and to you, I say this about fame: Do good work and good deeds. Treat your friends and your clients well. Solve their problems, provide for their needs, and give them good value. Do good work first, and then promote the heck out of it! Be famous for being the best at what you do and the way you do it. Market well your legitimate claim to fame, and only then will you have achieved fame that is truly desirable and sustainable.

In business, a well-crafted, diligently-guarded, and creatively-promoted brand will become famous for all the right reasons.

Visibility COACH The Visibility Coach says: Let others have their mere 15 minutes. You're in this for the long haul.

Ligers Among Us

"Hey Dad, look at this," my then five-year-old son Spencer says, running into my home office and excitedly waving a piece of paper.

"Let me see, Buddy," I respond. "What is that?" I ask with genuine surprise.

"It's a Liger," he says proudly, recognizing that he knows something that Daddy doesn't. "It's a cross between a lion and a tiger. Isn't it cool?"

"How do they do that?" I ask my little animal lover.

"God just takes a tiger and a lion," he explains, "and he squishes them together." He illustrates this by scrunching his face and pressing his hands together.

"Awesome!" I reinforce, as he runs off to go print more pictures.

For the undoctrinated, Ligers are the offspring of a male lion and female tiger (tigress). (For future reference, male tigers and female lions create Tigons. Not as common, but true nonetheless.)

What is truly amazing about Ligers is their sheer size. Far bigger and more impressive than either of their biological parents, Ligers are the largest of all the great cats, standing as tall as 10 feet on their hind legs and weighing a thousand pounds. Beyond simply surpassing their parents in scale, Ligers can do things that their parents can't or won't. For instance, unlike their lion fathers, Ligers love to swim.

The point is—and there *is* a point here—that there are strong parallels between the business world and the animal kingdom. In many instances, a legitimate case can be made for seeking out and partnering with others who can bolster our reach, expand our offerings, and enhance our value proposition. In doing so, we too can become greater than the sum of our parts—more attractive to prospective customers and more valuable to our current ones.

Remember the old TV commercials where the guy is walking with the chocolate bar and stumbles into the other guy with the jar of peanut butter? "Hey, you got chocolate on my peanut butter!" "And you got peanut butter on my chocolate!" Voila! Reese's Peanut Butter Cups were born.

Are there others in the marketplace that you could work with to combine forces to be more visible, credible, and attractive to your mutual prospects? Do you have a slice of the pie that, if combined with the other slices, could help you to offer more comprehensive services, cradle-to-grave coverage, or one-stop shopping?

While I am a huge proponent of specialization, opportunities often exist for partnering with complementary, synergistic, and mutually beneficial market players to help both or all of you look more impressive, more credible, and more capable. This potential synergy is the catalyst for a great number of strategic business acquisitions and partnerships that occur in the world today.

It's the large grass farm that buys a landscape installation company; the web development company that partners with an SEO boutique operation; and the slew of dispersed free-lancers that combine forces in a virtual model to bolster their capabilities in seeking to work with larger companies.

Are their others who don't do what you do, but sell to the same markets? Are you a lion who could become a Liger? Start sniffing around.

Postscript: Later that evening, my son charged into the family room triumphantly holding what he proclaimed to be his "favorite Liger picture ever!" My wife and I begin to stammer and we struggled to contain our laughter as he showed us a full-color picture of a liger and a tiger doing, well . . . what comes naturally. "She's giving him a piggy-ride!" he explains. "Yes, she is," we agree.

Visibility COACH   The Visibility Coach says: Don't settle for roaming the forest, competing with all other lions and tigers for fresh meat. Be a Liger and get the kill by being more impressive and powerful than your competition.

Are You Newsworthy?

Not surprisingly, one of the most common requests I hear from my clients is: "Can you get me on Oprah?" Well, since the Oprah show rarely considers unsolicited pitches from the outside world, no one can promise to deliver *that* holy grail.

So here's a secret that's not so secret: The best way to increase your chances of getting on Oprah, or any of the other coveted TV programs, is to be so good at what you do, so differentiated from your competitors, so well identified as an expert or leader in your unique category, and so well-established on the national level that Oprah FINDS YOU!

Many business owners and professionals spend so much time wondering "How do I get the word out about my expertise, business, or product" that they fail to ask the simple question: "Am I truly newsworthy?"

What unique category have you created for yourself? What is your distinctive mind-share? Best-selling author John Gray didn't tell the world that men and women approach relationships in a different way. We already knew that, didn't we? No, John Gray explained that *Men are from Mars and Women are from Venus.* That's *his* concept. It's his brand. He owns it.

When someone says "Amazon" you think of books. When they speak of the Tour de France you think of Lance Armstrong. When they say "that Subway guy" you think of Jared.

What are you known for? What do you own in the public's mind? What is your unique twist or approach to solving some problem that people readily identify with you? Remember, you have to own it before you promote it, or your customers won't remember you. Moreover, you have to have built a measure of success before the news media will take notice. You have to become *worthy* of their attention.

Remember that the news media is not your marketing department. You have to present something that fits within the parameters of their broadcast, publication, or web audience.

So here's your challenge: Craft a marketing approach to promoting your business that bears little resemblance to your competition. Devise and distinguish a mantra that is uniquely yours. Create a moniker that is descriptive, evocative, profound, and unique. Then live up to it. You'll be amazed how much more effective your publicity campaign can be when you become truly newsworthy.

Visibility **COACH**   The Visibility Coach says: If other people don't know who you are, how can you expect that Oprah will?

Be Found

One of the most fascinating movies I've ever seen was during a visit to the National Air and Space Museum at the Smithsonian in Washington, D.C. The short film, made over 30 years ago, was called *The Power of Ten* and was only eight minutes long, but it was profound in both its presentation and message.

The film began by showing a couple on a blanket in a park and zoomed out progressively every 10 seconds to 10 times the distance. You see very quickly how small the Earth is; eventually, how small our galaxy is; and then how astonishingly small and insignificant we all are in the overall cosmos, surrounded by a squillion other planets and galaxies.

At the time of writing this book, there are nearly 120 million web sites online with dozens of billions of web pages. (Oh, by the way—yours is one of them.)

In the early days of the Internet, having your own web site gave you a competitive advantage in the marketplace. It was, for most, merely an online brochure. The information was the same as that in your printed marketing materials—except now it was backlit! The real value for your customers was that the web site gave instant access to company information, 24/7.

With a web page, gone was the need to incur the expense of printing and mailing material detailing your product offerings or service. But once others started gravitating toward the Web, you were told that you needed to stand out online by having colorful graphics and mini-flash animation intros to tell your story and make you seem "cutting edge." More recently, the leading players have recognized the value of interactivity and e-commerce capabilities so that customers have the ability to purchase products and services at all hours of the day and night. The Web activity always grows and expands.

But along with the plethora of commercial and noncommercial web sites choking the Internet, a bigger challenge has emerged for business owners—being found. A colleague of mine has commented that putting up a web site is like building a business out in the middle of nowhere. I would assert that it's just the opposite: It's like building your business on an obscure side street in the heart of the biggest city the world has ever known. Everyone can easily get to you; finding you is another matter. You need to tell them where you are.

A well-known saying asserts that if you build a better mousetrap, the world will beat a path to your door. This no longer applies in the world of the Web. Now, please don't confuse sharing a proliferation of ideas on the Web with your web site. They are very different things. Ideas can go viral. Disturbing video clips, funny pictures, e-mailed hoaxes, and inappropriate jokes can spread like wildfire. Web sites don't spread. You have to be found.

Building an outstanding, graphically interesting, easy-to-navigate, content-rich web site accomplishes nothing if it is hard to find. Once again, I'm not talking about the ideal prospects that are already looking for you online and accurately type your domain name into their Internet browser or your exact name into the search engine. Those are the low-hanging fruit. I'm referring to the countless customers and prospects (possibly from all around the world) who don't know who you are, but are looking to buy what you're selling. How do they find you? How do they sift through the hundreds of millions of sites to zero-in on you?

The simple answer, of course, is that they will merely look on Google, Yahoo! Bing, or any one of the dozen strong search engines. So where do you come up in the search rankings? If someone were to type in your industry, the names of the products or service you offer (without using your specific name)—where do you pop up on the page? What? You're not on the first page? Do you even show up on the first hundred pages? Thousand, million pages? What are you doing to raise your be-found ability online?

You may or may not be familiar with the process of search engine optimization (SEO) or the discipline of search engine marketing (SEM), but you'd better bone-up quickly. Why? Because chances are your competition has already started down that road. In fact, if you want to know who has an active SEM program in place, search the terms that are standard for your business or industry and see whose web sites come up on the first page in the Google or Yahoo search results. Very little of that first-page ranking has to do with luck.

Why is this important? Because most shoppers will find what they want on that first page and never even make it to the second. How often do you keep shopping after you've found what you want?

"But my company is better!" you assert. "We can take care of the customer better or provide a better product or service!" Go ahead and keep talking. Stomp your foot if you need to. I can't hear you anyway. In fact, I'll never hear you or consider your company because I will never know you exist. Your web site is lost in a cyber-void, nestled between a 14-year-old girl's MySpace page and her online rant about how "Jenny is a total back-stabber" and a web site dedicated to organic gardening—in Malaysia.

The first page results on search engines gets almost all of the clicks and the majority of the business. The cruel reality is that the placement they achieve—and subsequent business they receive—has nothing to do with the quality of their products or even their market share. It has everything to do with how visible they are to the search engines, and how deliberate and strategic they are in the words they include on their web sites and how they present themselves to the "spiders."

Can I teach you to become an expert on all the intricacies of search engine optimization? Probably not, because I'm not very good at it. But I know who is. The good news is there are plenty of books, articles, and professionals who are good at it—and some are great. You can go as far down that road as you can afford, but you have to do something, lest you languish on Google's page 26,719—two-thirds of the way down.

What's the point of building a business if no one ever visits you – either physically or virtually? Optimize your online presence and be found!

Visibility COACH   The Visibility Coach says: There's a big difference between being "searchable" and being "findable!"

Your Expertise Is Boring

I see your lips moving, but all I hear is "Blah, blah, blah, blah, blah." I know it's not what you want me to hear, but quite simply, if you are a leader (or aspiring leader) in your industry—one who is frequently interviewed by the news media—your expertise just isn't very interesting. In fact—I hate to break it to you—information is a dime-a-dozen, and yours is no different.

So in this age of round-the-clock, on-demand, blue-tooth, online, high-def., Wi-Fi, via-satellite, news-junky, 3-G, out-of-home, at-your-fingertips world of information, what separates the messages that break through the clutter and the critical mass of opinions and expertise that go unnoticed? The answer is very simple: It's the delivery!

Information that is delivered by experts in a credible, but straightforward fashion is too-often reminiscent of a classroom lecture—boring! Perspective that is disseminated through a causal, respectful, but otherwise uneventful on-camera conversation is forgettable. However, that same content—those same opinions, delivered with passion, purpose, urgency, confidence, spirit, and edge-of-your-seat conviction, can move people to action and move you to the top of the news media's first call list.

The information stored in your brain is merely the entry fee for the big stage. Your credentials to deliver that content are only the prerequisite to gaining an audience with a reporter or producer. But your crusade is what truly makes you interesting. Your passion for the message is what makes you believable, and its timely connection to some current or personal challenge is what makes you relevant.

Watch any national morning or cable news/talk show and note who receives the lion's-share of camera time and the longer news segments. Most often, it's the person who takes control of the conversation. In television news, the one who steps up, unabashedly espouses his or her opinions, and most deftly steers the conversation, wins.

But all too often, experts who are invited to comment or offer perspective on a current story of national interest, blow the opportunity by merely answering the questions posed to them. They do a respectable job and their friends, family, and colleagues shower them with praise. But the reaction from the producer or reporter is tempered. After the segment or interview, the guest is likely complimented and graciously thanked for their time, but rarely asked back. Why? Because most media opportunities are a test in disguise. And most company leaders and subject experts unknowingly fail that test. Quite simply, their performance, while credible, was forgettable. They were boring.

But consider, for a moment, the experts that have been featured time and time again in the national news—some even being rewarded with their own show. Think Nancy Grace, Rush Limbaugh, Dr. Laura, James Carville, Dennis Miller, Dr. James Dobson, Celebrity Attorney Gloria Allred, Kanye West, and Glenn Beck. What do they have in common? The common trait they all share is that they are fiercely opinionated. They have strong convictions, disagree with the opposite perspective, know what they want to say and aren't afraid to say it. In many cases, they're paid to say it! I'm not suggesting that you have to be a jerk or overly controversial to be newsworthy, only that you have to have the confidence of conviction that personifies a true thought-leader.

Good radio talk show hosts, for example, don't bring up a topic neutrally and calmly, discuss both sides of the argument, and ask you to call and offer your opinions. No. Instead they tell you, in no uncertain terms, what they think and invite you to agree or disagree. Who among us would be inspired to follow or be moved to action by a merely credible, straightforward expert offering his or her fact-laden expertise on a story of national or industry-specific interest?

To build your visibility, attract clients or customers, inspire others to hire you or buy your products, engender loyalty, and inspire true change—you must move beyond the realm of simply being smart and capable. You must truly *inspire*.

And while we are all made up of the same composite materials, each of us is wired a little differently. Being overly expressive and delivering content on the edge of your seat can be challenging for some, but it must be done if you are going to be seen as a leader in your space. In working with the news media, we are playing in *their* sandbox and we must meet their standards and play by their rules, or we won't be asked to play again.

Visibility COACH   The Visibility Coach says: Memorable people and brands aren't boring. Don't be boring.

Reach Out and Re-Touch Someone

It's a reality that every business faces: there will be good months and there will be not-so-good months. Basic economics dictate that the key to profitability and survival in business is to ensure that the good months outnumber the bad ones. For small businesses, this fact is even more crucial as you (we) tend to lack the infrastructure and substantial financial reserves to weather extended downturns in the economy.

So how do you help to ensure that the good times continue all year long? You have to find a way to remain top-of-mind with your top prospects. You know the old 20-80 rule, which suggests that 80 percent of your revenue is going to come from 20 percent of your clients. The lesson is: While you are always prospecting for new business, never lose sight of the importance of keeping visible with your current clients and key contacts.

Since the vast majority of my business comes from referrals, I always make a concerted effort to connect and reconnect with those I know, and those who know me. I generally don't put out an overt call for business, but rather always work to keep my name, face, and voice front-and-center with my important connections and business relationships.

Small business expert and author Mark LeBlanc speaks about the importance of connecting with your "advocates." He urges people to find a reason to reach out to the important personal and professional relationships in their life at least once a month. He doesn't suggest asking for work, but simply sending a newspaper clipping or e-mail relevant to their business, making a lunch date, calling to check-in, sending a business referral, and so on. The goal is to move yourself from the back of their minds to the front of their minds.

Business relationship guru David Nour speaks and con-
sults with organizations about how to cultivate, craft, bolster, and nurture strategic business connections. He teaches
professionals how to move beyond traditional networking
and really focus on what it takes to build truly meaningful
bonds, and to do so without any expectation of financial
gain. We know that people do business with people they
like, and they like people who do things for them. Nour's
tele-seminars on LinkedIn and other business social networking sites are not only eye-opening, but truly business-
transforming.

With all this wonderful wisdom in-hand, recently I set out
on a "re-connect with Dave" campaign. I quadrupled my social network connections. I reached out to all my Skype Internet phone colleagues around the world, and I even sent
"What's up" messages to old friends, co-workers, classmates
and others—just to say "hi."

The results? Many were glad to hear from me and were
curious about my life, my kids, and my business. I had a great
time reconnecting with old friends, and I learned that many
previous clients and colleagues had moved, changed jobs, or
embarked on exciting new ventures. I discovered that becoming top-of-mind with my current connections brought about a
slew of new business opportunities for which I would not
likely have been considered because I simply would not have
come to mind as an option.

Through this easy and rewarding exercise of reaching out
and reconnecting with old colleagues, clients and friends, my
traditionally slower time of year was transformed into one of
my most active. I signed on a number of new clients and
booked numerous speaking gigs across America and around

the world—all from individuals I already knew, but whom I had not been in contact with for some time.

Remember, augmenting your visibility doesn't always have to be on the macro level to be effective.

Visibility COACH   The Visibility Coach says: Sometimes it can be more valuable to be top-of-mind with people who already know and like you than with the thousands who you hope will.

Don't Be a Twit

At this point, you probably don't need to be informed about the growing adoption, prevalence, and acceptance of social media in our lives. You've likely been educated (or hounded) about the importance of participating in social media, and barraged with the potential benefits to your business. However, as happens to all concepts that are still in their infancy, some people will tend to misuse them. Since this book is not really a how-to guide—and since much of what I say about this subject will be obsolete before it is even printed—I won't attempt to expose, only illustrate.

Those who originally envisioned and pioneered social media portals like MySpace and Facebook saw a way for people to connect with new friends while reconnecting with old ones. The Twitter folks saw a way, though micro-blogging, to share short notes, thoughts, and updates in order to stay connected with faraway friends. As is true with all new ideas, widespread adoption requires—and often drives—a shift in thoughts and behaviors. It's all extremely fascinating, and it can be a lot of fun – or truly annoying – depending on your perspective.

Of course, with all new communication mediums, others will see the opportunity to utilize the new conduit to market their wares to anyone and everyone they can reach. Spam (not the luncheon meat) will always be hot on the heels of any better mousetrap created to facilitate and expedite communication. It is rumored that when the first two tin cans were connected with a piece of string, one of the first messages involved a pitch for low-cost health insurance.

What is disturbing is to notice how many professionals are jumping in the muck right along with the much-reviled spammers. Okay, maybe their pitches are not quite as overt, but they are almost as prevalent. In fact, the vast majority of Facebook posts and Twitter "Tweets" that I receive from professional colleagues are suggestions and invitations to visit their blog, attend their boot camp, buy their supplements, and join their "fan-group."

To answer some critics: Yes, it is boring to tell us what kind of cereal you are eating for breakfast each day, but trying to get me to give you my money—over Twitter—is downright offensive.

Skip, skip, delete, skip, delete. Occasionally, I will even see some I want to read. Why, from time to time, I might actually see something interesting. Hey, Joe is stuck at an airport in Prague. (What was he doing in Prague?) Jeffrey is going to the Oscars. (Lucky dude has some very cool perks in his job at Kodak.) Paula is opening her new day spa in Texas. (She did it!) Barb ate some bad clams. (Been there.) David's daughter was leading scorer on her basketball team. (Second year in a row!)

Do we really care? I say we do—*if*. We will care if you make the effort to truly connect with us and cause us to care. Unfortunately, too many don't yet get the real power and potential of the micro-blogging medium. Too many populate the extremes of the spectrum by either relating the mundane (hmmm, buying tube-socks are we? Fascinating), or the marketing pitch (no, I don't want to click on the article touting the remarkable new diet formula you've developed).

Then how do we, as unapologetic, capitalist business owners and professionals, embrace this new medium without falling into the "market ourselves anywhere we can" trap? It starts with a recognition that we're more likely to do business with people who like us and feel connected to us. It's true that people like people who are like them. All things being equal (and we can never let them be equal!), when you share a bit of yourself, the right people will feel a sense of connection with you.

When I post updates, it is most often to help my "friends" and those "following me" connect with me. I want them to feel that they really know me as a person. It's fascinating that the majority of responses I receive to a Facebook or Twitter post come when I make fun of myself, when I make slice-of-life observations about my wife and kids, or lament the trials and tribulations of being a busy Dad. People relate to that and are inspired to join the conversation. Will they feel like they know my competitors as they know me, on a personal level? Not likely—unless my competitors do the same thing.

Your updates can also help to position you and your business without overtly boasting about your success. When I comment in a Facebook or Twitter post about the fact that

I'm dreading the 19-hour flight to Singapore for a speaking engagement—or that I just drank a phenomenal beer in Antwerp—I want those reading to think: "Wow! He's got gigs all over the world! He must be a big deal." It's not ego; it's positioning and visibility. It's a means to an end—and it works.

When someone comments about how exhausted they are after working all day and night at their "packed" grand opening, they've just told everyone that they have a new location that is now open. They didn't try to sell anyone anything, but may end up selling a great deal for those that come to shop at the new location. Transparent? Not necessarily. For many of us, our business is an integral part of our lives; if we can make our communications interesting and somewhat revealing, we can connect and promote without offending.

Take a moment to think: Is there a purpose to this post or update to your social media site? Is what you're doing, thinking, or planning likely to be regarded as interesting or relevant to others? Are you blatantly marketing, or are you sharing, connecting, and enlightening your "friends?"

We are all busy and bristle at the thought of adding any new activity or obligation to our overflowing plate. But think of social media not as something else to do, but as doing what you're already doing, differently.

Visibility COACH The Visibility Coach says: Social media is here to stay. Abuse it and you'll just bother or alienate people. Use it wisely and you can build relationships that can help build your network – and your business.

Fame by Association

I was sitting in a movie theater with a friend a few years ago, waiting for the show to start and watching the string of local merchant advertising slides that were keeping us entertained. A slide appeared on the big screen promoting a local pediatric dentist and my friend started to laugh. He explained his laughter, noting that he knew the woman in the ad since she was pretty notorious in the local networking and dating scene.

The ad touted her expertise and the focus of her dental practice. Then—in big letters across the bottom—it featured the magic words that so many in business and most authors covet most of all. It is the holy grail of advertising claims. There, big, bright, and bold on the screen it said: "As seen on Oprah!"

Wow. This local dentist was a guest on *Oprah*. In one simple statement, she just leaped above all area competitors in credibility and visibility because she connected herself and her industry know-how with the queen of American television and one of our most influential public figures, especially when it comes to a very important demographic—Moms. She was on Oprah! She must be good.

My friend shook his head in disbelief, explaining that the unspoken truth in her claim was that she was indeed a guest on Oprah, but not for her dental expertise. She was a guest on a show that was featuring self-described "gold-diggers"— women who won't date a man unless he can show her his platinum American Express card!

Regardless of how you feel about the ethics and the implications in her Oprah reference, it speaks to a larger issue of credibility gained through media exposure. I had a client for whom I helped secure an appearance on Good Morning America some years back. Through a pre-taped story and local interview commenting on youth behavior for the Great American Smoke-Out, his total on-screen time was about six seconds. But now he can tout his national exposure and casually state in person and in his marketing efforts: "Perhaps you saw me on *Good Morning America.*"

This dynamic is at the core of the distinction between marketing and public relations. When you advertise, you are expected to say great things about yourself. We all know the game. In commercials and other ads, you boast about how soft your product is, how delicious your food tastes, and how clean you smell. You get exposure, for sure, but it's tempered with the recognition that the message is bought and paid for.

But it's far more credible when a national news media outlet or local business news source extols your virtues by devoting screen time or column inches to you. *That's* public relations. "Don't listen to me," you say in answer to a doubting challenge from a prospective customer. "Just read what they said about us in the *Wall Street Journal.*" That's powerful.

As most customers are looking for a safe choice and a good decision, press coverage can bolster your credibility and be the tipping point in helping you land business. In a vast sea of competitors, sometimes it takes very little to stand out. Connecting yourself, your message, and product to a major name or news source can help you become the 800-pound gorilla.

Get press, even if it's a small mention, and ride that baby all the way.

Visibility COACH   The Visibility Coach says: If others are talking about you, then you must be good!

Good TV

There has been a dramatic shift in television media content in the twenty-first century and, ironically, it's been a shift *away* from the dramatic. Expensive, scripted television has been in decline in favor of "reality" programs, competitions, and prime-time game shows. From *American Idol*, *Survivor*, and *Dancing with the Stars*, to *America's Next Top Model*, *The Biggest Loser*, *The Hills*, and *Deal or No Deal*—"reality" reigns supreme.

But how real are the contestants and participants? I'm not suggesting that the lines are scripted, or alluding to any kind of game-show scandal. But what is clear is that the contestant selection process is conducted with a clear agenda in mind—good TV. From the over-the-top, border-line-spastic game show contestant; the no-talent, but painfully unaware singing hopeful; to the intentionally exacerbated roommate conflict—these "real people" bear little resemblance to the real people in your life. But while some may argue that this barrage of guilty pleasure, filter-through-your-fingers window into the lives of people you would never be friends with is good TV—few would argue the benefits to the sponsors.

So how does the issue of good TV (or good other media) translate into opportunities to raise your profile or build your business? To achieve a level of beneficial, high profile media sustainability, you've got to provide them the journalistic version of good TV.

New, innovative, or provocative solutions to long-standing problems can be good TV. Healthy, but spirited exchanges or outright conflict among expert guests can both be good TV. Good TV means nothing more than being interesting and not blending in. Unfortunately, experts tend to be so immersed in their content that they believe it is the information that is interesting, when in reality it is the passion that brings about good TV.

The biggest misperception in working with the press is the notion that when reporters ask a question, it is because they want to know the answer. That is rarely the case. Unless you are the subject or point-person for a criminal or news investigation, the purpose of the reporter's questions, in most cases, is simply to provide a launch pad for your ideas, input, and perspective. I'm not suggesting that you don't answer the question being posed, but rather that you recognize that your response should be used as the springboard for your crusade.

Here's the key to a good media interview: Most reporters don't know the subject nearly as well as the guest. So when a reporter asks you something, answer it briefly and transition into what you really went there to talk about. You can expertly move past the often irrelevant or less important question by simply employing transitional phrases. For example:

"While I certainly agree, it's also important to remember that . . ."

"I understand what you're saying, but the issue that really concerns me is . . ."

"While that issue is making headlines, we can't forget that . . ."

"Well, that may be true in the past, let me give you a good sense of where we are today . . ."

"Thanks for asking. First let me say that I really appreciate . . ."

"People sometimes fail to recognize that . . ."

"I find it fascinating that . . ."

Then go on to say what you came there to say, and do it with passion, regardless of the questions asked. If the reporter has something else in mind, don't worry—they'll jump in. Get on the edge of your seat and advocate for your position, organization, product, or crusade, and do it as if you only have one minute to make your case (because that's likely all you *do* have), and keep talking!

Since most on-air interviews last no more than a minute or two, I advise my clients to be crystal clear in their mind what they want to say, what they must say, and what is crucial for them to impart to the audience if they are to be successful in their business. Then they must make a solemn pledge to themselves (and to me) that they will not get out of that chair until they say it!

It's the quid pro quo of working with the press: We help them fill up their newspapers and newscasts with (good) content, and in return we get a platform to relay our ideas. Use it. Don't waste it. Don't be boring. Be opinionated. Be passionate, relevant, provocative, believable, timely, different, memorable, and newsworthy. That's good TV and that's what will get you asked back again and again.

Give them a great interview. Give them your whole heart and soul and worry more about your mission and message than their questions. Despite conventional wisdom, the reporter or interviewer will be very appreciative of your media savvy and recognition of what their real need is in this encounter—and it's not the answer to simple questions. It's good TV.

Visibility COACH The Visibility Coach says: There are hundreds of millions of TV remote controls and page-turning fingers out there. Be interesting and they'll likely stick with you, turn to you, and come back to you. Be boring and . . . . Click.

Care for a Sample?

Saturday is a big day for my kids and they are always giddy with anticipation. On many a Saturday, my family is presented with the opportunity to dine on a vast array of flavors and textures from across the country and around the world. Saturday is the day they get to partake in one of the biggest smorgasbords consistently offered in the free world. Yes, my friends—all too often, Saturday is Costco day.

For the uninitiated, Costco features food vendors (represented by a veritable crap-shoot of friendly or ill-tempered "servers") offering free samples of their products to passersby. Armed with either a hot plate or portable microwave oven, these servers prepare bite-sized trials of dinner items, seafood recipes, fruit wedges, and even health drinks. Yum!

While these giveaways no doubt come with a cost to the manufacturers, the concept is simple—and proven: You can't have a repeat customer until you have a first-time customer.

"Yes, I would like one of those! Thank you. Those delicious Tyson Buffalo Wings are right behind you in the frozen food? And that big bag is only $8.99; and they just need to be heated and served? Sure, I'll take a bag!" Unless, of course, my wife makes me put them back.

The benefits of sampling cut across all industries: It's a test drive at the local car dealership. It's a money-back guarantee from a mail order house, or a free consultation with the local chiropractor. Sampling (pause to take a deep breath) is a toothpick surrounded by a saucy morsel of awesome Orange Chicken goodness from Panda Express at the mall food court (and . . . exhale).

When all in business profess quality, how are prospective customers or clients supposed to know how good you really are—until they work with you, try your coffee, see your facility, or brush a sample of your paint on the wall of their baby's nursery? While not all industries lend themselves well to the concept of offering free samples (diamond jewelry dealers come to mind), most do offer legitimate opportunities to showcase your product, or some mechanism for lessening the risk to consumers of choosing to purchase.

Keep in mind that you don't need to give away a free sample of your product or service to achieve the same benefit of awareness and familiarization. A construction company specializing in basement finishing isn't likely to build you a free bathroom to see if you like their work, but they can easily show you samples of their previous projects to demonstrate the quality of their design and construction. Their samples can be presented in a colorful brochure or even as a virtual tour via their web site accompanied by a long list of satisfied customers.

In my speaking business, for example, there is no shortage of presenters vying for the same stage time at conferences and conventions. Ultimately, clients are seeking a sense of confidence that the speaker they choose will be able to deliver strong content and be well received by their audience. I know that without the opportunity to view a preview of me actually speaking to an audience, every other thing I do to promote my business will fall short.

Of course, it's unrealistic to expect that prospective clients will travel to some far-off city to watch me speak, or that they will actually take the time to leave work or home and come to where I might be speaking close to their hometown. Armed with that reality, I make it as easy as possible for prospects to sample my work—right on their computer screen.

On my web site home page, and on most of my other web pages as well, a clickable screen is right there, up front and prominently placed: *"Watch David Avrin's Preview Video!"* beckons the prospects. I don't make them search for it or scroll through any drop-down menu to find it.

Is anyone going to hire me to speak to their organization without a chance to sample my work? Not likely.

How about you? I'm sure your current customers love you, but what about those that have yet to be brought on board? Is there a way, beyond the delivery of your traditional marketing messages and efforts to provide a sample of what you do, what you have done, and what you could do for them? Let them experience a sample, a snippet or sense of what you offer and you will reduce the fear-factor substantially. Seeing is believing.

"Bourbon chicken? Sure, I'll take one. Uh, can I get an extra one for my wife? She's around here somewhere."

Visibility COACH   The Visibility Coach says: Don't make them wonder what your work looks like, tastes like, or feels like. Give them a sample and become the safe choice to make.

Pal Around

There's a famous parable that has a man on his hands and knees under a streetlamp after dark, apparently searching the ground for a lost item. A guy walks by and says:

"What'cha lookin' for?"

"My keys," the guy responds.

"Ya lose 'em over here?" the guy asks.

"No. Actually I lost them over there," the man says, pointing off to his right, "but the light is better here."

Are you looking for love in all the wrong places? Where are your best prospects? Where do they congregate? Where do they connect with each other? Where do they meet, gather, dine, live, and shop? And more important—are you there too?

Some professionals bristle at the thought of joining local Chambers of Commerce, leads groups, or professional associations, but others wouldn't dream of doing business without them. While certain models work better for my business than others, I recognize the vast potential and value of all of them. In fact, the new concepts and organizations that don't work for their members fall quickly by the wayside. The ones that survive and thrive likely provide tremendous value for the right professionals.

The best jobs are never posted or advertised, the biggest business deals are forged in a back booth at a restaurant, on the golf course, or in the lounge of a private club. Often the best sales opportunities are referred by a friend or colleague.

Do you have a strong professional network? Do you know influential people in your industry (or in your prospects' industry) and do they know you?

Let's be clear: I am referring to more than simply passing out your business card or overtly asking for business. I am looking toward building a true network of business relationships and friendships, of putting your personal and professional brand "out there."

Professional associations, by and large, are a must for business owners and working professionals. They are the best way to keep current on industry happenings, challenges, innovations, opportunities, and trends. While there is often a measure of posturing and gamesmanship, the cost of being out-of-the-loop can be profound. How can you best differentiate yourself in a crowded marketplace if you are not well-versed on the practices and approach of your competitors? How can you achieve a beneficial level of visibility in the marketplace if you are not visible within your own industry or local market?

Enjoying the fruits of these relationships requires more than simply paying for your membership and receiving the newsletter. You must be present at scheduled meetings, actively reach out to colleagues, attend industry conferences, and actually read the information sent to you.

The real benefits of association memberships often reveal themselves when you go above and beyond your membership requirements and become active and visible within the organization. Volunteering for committees and additional duties makes you stand out and be seen as a "doer" and leader in your industry. Your position on professional boards-of-directors and other leadership positions gives you national standing and great credibility. This helps you not only gain visibility in your industry, but credibility among prospects.

Some of the most profoundly valuable connections come from membership and participation in CEO organization and small groups. I am proud to serve as a group chair with Vistage International (formerly known as TEC), the world's leading chief executive organization. In my group leadership role, I see first-hand the power that connecting and sharing with peers can provide. Unlike professional associations, CEO groups like Vistage bring together a dozen or more company leaders—all from different industries—to discuss, explore, prod, question, and help solve the personal and organizations challenges of their fellow members. It's not a networking group, but a coming together of leaders faced with the similar challenges of building their businesses and weathering difficult economic times. The business referrals that inevitably occur are not part of the process, but simply a natural byproduct of the connections members feel with others that they "go to war with" each month. It's awesome!

Other fine organizations like YPO, EO, LeTip, C-12, NAWBO, Forty Plus, and others, provide opportunities to rub shoulders, explore issues, listen to speakers, break bread, and share leads.

Imagine that your head is encased in a 12-inch cube. Everything you know is in that cube. All that you have learned and thought in your life, the wisdom born of your unique experiences, is all located inside that cube. Of course, everything that you don't know is outside that cube. Pal around with others who are looking to expand their cube as well.

Visibility COACH   The Visibility Coach says: Connect with others who've been there and are still doing that.

Picture Yourself

Close your eyes. Picture a cute, chubby little baby. Now imagine that same baby with sunflower petals around her head sitting inside a flower pot. Bing! A name just came to your mind. Might that name be Anne Geddes?

Now imagine a grand piano, every inch of it covered by small, mirrored tiles. Picture a candelabra sitting atop the piano and a man with a long purple cape, all covered with sequins. The over-60 set will easily think of the flamboyant Liberace.

Think of a car shaped like a giant hot dog; an old European tower leaning to one side; a giant purple dinosaur singing children's songs; an opera house shaped like giant ship sails; an island wrapped in pink plastic; and a cartoon mouse with a broad smile and big, round black ears.

You can picture these things, can't you? We are visual beings and some of the most enduring icons of our lives and business brands have seared very recognizable images into our brains. It's the hideous, menacing face and knife-like fingers of Freddie Krueger; the powerfully stark image of the long black slabs engraved with a seemingly endless list of names on the Vietnam Memorial; the puffed-out cheeks of Louis

Armstrong; the Golden Arches of McDonalds; the distinctive, soft texture of Jim Henson's Muppets; and the familiar swoosh of . . . well. you know who has the swoosh.

The point is that the visual aspect of your brand can play a large role in how, and if, you are remembered. After the launch of your company, have you spent much time truly considering the images that represent your business and brand? They can include your logo or service mark, but also the look and feel of your physical location, the uniforms your staff may wear, the mascot or character that you put forward, and the packaging of your products. Perhaps your brand is linked to the image of your first product, the one that launched your company like Pixar's personality-infused lamp. Maybe it's the face of your founder (Colonel Sanders) or the distinctive look of your signature (Disney) or your signature product (iPod).

What image can you put forward and promote that, in a split second, says . . . you? Just like the importance of using words that don't mirror those of your competitors, think of images that connect your prospects' minds to you and only you, and use them consistently in your marketing efforts.

Visibility COACH   The Visibility Coach says: Can your customers and prospects identify you at a glance?

Is Your Voice Viral?

What do your kids' germs, the worst music video ever produced, (http://www.youtube.com/watch?v=YPnGPIMUnus), Susan Boyle's performance on Britain's Got Talent, and Bill

Gates's purported graduation speech have in common? They've all spread like a virus.

The best and the worst of the Internet can "go viral" and it's a condition to which you should aspire. It's not simply identifying a new trend; going viral means that an online item—a video clip, essay, or some other nugget of wisdom or entertainment—is so captivating that millions of people not only want to watch it, but are motivated to pass it on to others. It's the difference between idle chatter and juicy gossip; between hitting the delete button and claiming that "you gotta see this!"

In the early days of the Web, it was often simply an off-color joke or an Internet hoax that seemed to show up in your e-mail box. In recent years, however, those simple pass-around-the-office nuggets have made way for sophisticated video parodies, online rants from disgruntled customers, and even thinly-veiled, but highly entertaining strategic marketing entries.

Many computer animation companies create funny online greeting cards, like the popular political parodies from Jib Jab and launch it into cyberspace for free in the hope that it will be passed around, providing exposure for the company.

One early phenomenon was launched by a terrific speaker and science guru Steve Spangler. A high-energy and wildly creative educator, Steve created the now-famous Mentos candy experiment as a way to help science teachers be amazing to their students. In the original video—and the myriad copies that have resulted—he drops an entire roll of Mentos candy into a two-liter bottle of Diet Coke, and an instantaneous volcano of soda squirts high into the air. It's very cool and visually stunning.

As a result of posting the video demonstration online, Spangler has received tens of millions of hits and millions of unique visitors to his company web site since 2007. And now, as you would expect, thousands of similar Mentos experiment videos have been posted online as well. When you Google the word "Mentos" today, Steve's personal web site—and the YouTube link pages—are always among the top five non-paid results. Ah, the value of viral.

Sometimes it is not simply a great visual, but the passing around of e-mails seeking and offering solutions or the widespread endorsement of a great resource that can go viral. Unfortunately, along with the valuable entries has come a glut of hoaxes, malicious computer viruses, and campaigns of mean-spirited and partisan misinformation aimed at shaping public opinion and, in turn, public policy.

The fact is that along with the explosive growth of the Web and the phenomenal access to valuable information has come an overwhelming glut of meaningless drivel. Okay, let's just call it what it is—crap! Simply posting ideas is no longer sufficient if building your business is the end game. Since virtually every 14-year-old girl in the world has her own web site, MySpace, or Facebook page—and countless homebound anarchists are blogging their incoherent rants on an hourly basis—it becomes all the more important to ensure that your insights are not simply taking up space, but are worthy of going viral in cyberspace.

Many of my coaching clients are in the information-sharing business (speakers, authors, consultants). And like the information we provide in our live presentations—or what I espouse in my coaching sessions—information intended for a cyber audience must be unique, profound, insightful, entertaining, and astoundingly timely and relevant.

Are you writing your e-zines and blogging simply because it is the day you are scheduled to write these things, or are you waiting until you have something truly relevant to say? There is a fine line between creating content to optimize your web site for the search engines and training your audience to ignore your overwhelming barrage of content; between using your webcam to talk about your business or hiring professionals to help showcase your business in a visually appealing and potentially entertaining way.

Remember the goal here: It's not just content for the sake of content, but information to capture the attention of your prospects. Wait until you have something to say that someone actually wants to hear! Look at your e-zines, e-mails, podcasts, promotional videos, blogs, and other online postings with a larger goal than simply getting it out there, but of producing content that is worthy of actually going viral.

Visibility COACH   The Visibility Coach says: Go big. Be wildly creative and astoundingly provocative, profound, and entertaining. If you're lucky, you may do more than simply and effectively market your business; you may actually go viral!

Black and White and Read All Over

Here's a quick question for you: What's the difference between someone who is very smart and someone who is a recognized expert in their field? Well, it could be that the latter has an advanced educational degree. It might even be that he or she has achieved a measure of fame or public accolades for a significant feat or discovery. The reality is that, for many, often the missing link between credibility and obscurity is simply having written and published a book.

Being the author of a book—on almost *any* subject—can make you an instant expert in your chosen category. Right or wrong, it's an interesting dynamic that plays itself out with decision makers every day. "Why is this person credible?" a meeting planner or television producer might ask a colleague. "Oh, he is the author of The Complete Guide to X" is often the response. "Sounds good. Get him on the phone."

Regardless of the content or subject matter, there is an unmistakable mystique that surrounds someone who has written a book. Like the woman who wears a white lab coat at the Clinique makeup counter in a major department store (with her apparent medical credentials), credibility can sometimes be a simple accessory away. A book can be that accessory.

Now, let me be clear: I'm not advocating cranking out a sloppy book or looking for a shortcut around earned credentials and true expertise. I'm merely highlighting the reality of our culture that allows for creative and legitimate means of bringing your hard-won expertise to the forefront. Write a book—gain the credibility. Write *the* book—gain fame and fortune.

The irony is that the book itself is rarely newsworthy. Unless you are blowing the lid off some current scandal or penning the tell-all memoir of a well-known politician or movie star, few people will truly care about the actual book. It's you, your message, and the subject matter that can earn you the spotlight to share your views. Having written the book can simply help you gain the platform.

Aside from the potential financial return from publishing your own book, the real payoff is in the doors a book can open. Experts who are also authors are more attractive to prospective clients, news producers, meeting planners, and so forth. A book makes you appear to be a safer choice. You must know what you're talking about—after all, you wrote a book on the subject!

I witnessed this firsthand when I wrote my own book: *The Gift in Every Day—Little Lessons on Living a Big Life* (Sourcebooks, 2006). This was a big departure from my marketing, PR, and branding work. I call it my "sappy dad" book. Now, let's be clear. I am not a certified life coach, parenting expert, psychologist, or any kind of credentialed guru on how to live a fulfilling life. I'm just a guy who decided to check in and take stock—and got my book published.

Because I went through the process of putting my thoughts on paper, I now have the opportunity—and great privilege— of speaking to thousands of people through media appearances (86 TV and radio to date) and keynote presentations on a subject about which I feel especially passionate. I don't offer myself as an expert; just an introspective and humorous guy with an important personal message to share about life, love, and making an impact on those around us. Would I have had the opportunity to speak (and get paid) about this subject had I not written a book? Not a chance!

Many of my coaching and consulting clients have a lifetime of expertise and wisdom that they share with their clients and audiences. Unfortunately, too many of their brilliant thoughts, insights, and solutions simply dissipate into thin air the moment the words leave their mouths. That's why it's important to get your thoughts down in the pages of a book, for so many reasons.

Of course, the biggest obstacle to writing is just getting started. It may sound overly simple, but the secret to writing is to *write*. One good way to get over the trepidation or to overcome the dreaded writer's block is to record your words, or have someone interview you and record the conversation. Then take the MP3 or other electronic file and send it off to a transcription service that will convert your recording into written text. Voila!—the beginning of a book. Now all you need to do is edit and enhance the manuscript.

There are many services available to help you get your book in print. With the rise of Amazon.com, a real book deal with a major publisher is no longer required to achieve national distribution. Print-on-demand makes small quantities afford-able and allows for simple and quick self-publication. There has never been an easier or less expensive time to self-publish.

There is a wonderful old African proverb that says: *"When an old person dies, a library burns to the ground."* Write the book and your wisdom lives on.

Visibility COACH   The Visibility Coach says: Don't take your knowledge with you. Share it in a tangible way and watch your visibility grow.

Get Yourself Booked

Because there are, on average, more than 1,000 books pub-lished in America every *day*, books are generally not news-worthy. News media outlets in America are inundated on a daily basis with press releases and media kits promoting newly published books. Some have even tried to stem the never-ending influx of press kits and releases by issuing a formal pol-icy against promoting new books.

Then how is it that so many authors end up in the pages of newspapers and being interviewed on television? The strategy is simple: Don't promote your book!

Now, let me be clear. The books are an integral part of the pitch and the hook, but books in and of themselves are not exciting. Of course, if you're J. K. Rowling, Donald Trump, John Grisham, or Stephen King, new books can create their own buzz, but for the rest of us books are a dime-a-dozen.

What *is* (potentially) newsworthy is the subject matter, your expertise, mission, and passion. What can grab attention is your profound take on a current subject making news, or your unique approach to solving a current or long-standing problem. The book merely adds to your credentials. Remember the following four points:

1. **The Hook is More Important Than the Book**—Make sure that the subject matter you're pitching is timely and relevant to your audience. Set about to creatively pitch the message of the book, with you as a crusader and expert touting an important message. The release of the book is the timely hook to promote that message.

2. **Perception Equals Reality**—One of the initial goals of any publicity campaign should be to achieve a slew of small successes on the local level, and use those media hits as leverage to garner larger opportunities. Here's how to do it: Every time you are able to do a live TV appearance or a phone-in radio segment, add that media hit to the long list of other hits on the News Media Coverage page of your book's web site – http://www.thegiftineveryday.com/newsmedia.html–thus creating a sense

that you are a hot commodity and media around the country are clamoring to talk to you.

Every time you contact a news reporter, producer, or program host with your well-prepared pitch, also send them a link to the media page on your web site and let them see for themselves that you are a big deal. Not only can they see all the articles in which you've been featured, they can also see the broadcast stations that clearly thought you were worth interviewing. It's a great third-party endorsement. Better yet, if you provide the links, or upload the media clips to YouTube, they can watch you being interviewed to erase any doubt that the segment would work well. Invariably, when I pitch in this way, I get a call back from the media prospect within minutes asking me to appear on their show.

3. **Take Your Message On the Road!**—I'm sure you've heard the saying, "You're never a prophet in your own land." The truth is that we're always a bigger deal when we come from somewhere else. Most speakers, consultants, coaches, authors, and other experts with books miss out on a wonderful opportunity for press that this phenomenon provides—the "visiting author" buzz.

Whenever I am traveling to speak or consult in another city, I play what I call the "Visiting Author Game." I always call ahead to the local press a couple of weeks out, and play up the fact that I am an author traveling to their city and am going to be in town "for just one day" promoting my new book and discussing the importance of X. I tell them that I will be doing an in-store appearance and book signing as well as "a ton" of local press. I then give them the opportunity to "have me first." Of course, I also give them a very strong pitch about the subject matter, and why their viewers, listeners, or readers would care. I also send them a link to my media page on the web site, in order to look as in-demand as possible.

After they book me to appear or schedule an interview, I then call a local book store and say that I am going to be doing a ton of local press and need a place to have a book signing and direct potential book buyers to during my TV interview. They don't want to miss out, so they schedule me and promote my in-store appearance. Even if I end up with only five people showing up at the store, I reach hundreds of thousands through the local press. As a bonus, the hits on my book web site go through the roof.

4. **Walk Before You Run**—Finally, too many author/ experts dream about being featured on the *Today* show, Jay Leno, Dr. Phil, or dare I say—Oprah. The odds are long, but it can be done. The reality is that producers from top national shows don't want to discover anything themselves; they have many thousands of experts to choose from. They also like to feature books, approaches, philosophies, experts, and crusaders whose messages have already caught fire. They want to jump on a train that is already hauling down the tracks, not one that is preparing to leave the station. Your goal should not be to get national press but to fan the local flames so that the fire spreads nationally. If you're successful, big media will find you.

Create small pockets of success and parlay those victories into bigger opportunities. Pitch the message of the book and yourself as the messenger—not the book itself. Tie the message to something on their agenda, and offer a new perspective or solution. And finally—create a way for others to see what you have achieved. Unless you've penned the next *Harry Potter* or *Purpose-Driven Life*, you're going to need to start small and fan the flames of success. As I always say, the greatest enemy of success in business (and publishing) is anonymity!

Visibility COACH   The Visibility Coach says: Write the book, but promote the hook.

See and Be Seen!

Some years back, I was attending a conference with my colleagues at the National Speakers Association and having fun zipping around the convention hotel on a Segway scooter. As I rounded a corner, I passed a woman who said, "Hey, I remember you!" "That's the point!" I said with a smile as I zoomed past.

For a time, the Segway was my schtick. I used to bring it along as my signature at conferences and conventions around the world. It was a great way to meet far more people than I normally would at such a large event. After all, as they say: "You can't be an introvert on a Segway!" Sometimes, there would even be a line of people in the lobby wanting to give it a try, and I was always happy to oblige.

More important, I always knew that I could call any of the hundreds or even thousands of fellow attendees in the weeks that followed and say, "I was the guy on the Segway." People would instantly recall who I was and the conversation was a breeze from there. If I'm going to call myself the Visibility Coach, I better be visible!

My question for you then is: "What are you doing to be noticed and remembered by your prospects?" Please don't get me wrong; I'm not suggesting that you have to find some hokey stunt to draw attention to yourself. But if there is a distinctive hook or activity that dovetails nicely into who you are or what you do, by all means, don't overlook it.

At that time, my Segway (personal transporter) was more than simply a great networking tool; it was also the centerpiece of my signature story, so it become my trademark. My wife shook her head and accused me of telling the Segway story on stage so I could justify buying one for myself. "Uh . . . so what's your point?" I responded.

What are *you* doing to be seen and remembered? How are you ensuring your top-of-mind status with your clients and prospects?

One exercise I conduct with my clients is to ask them the question, "Who cares about your business?" It's not a flippant or dismissive query. I'm dead serious. Who cares about what you offer? Who needs to know who you are for you to be successful? Better yet, who in your target markets needs to know you, what you do, what you offer, and what makes you different?

Open your laptop or get a paper and pen and start a list. First, jot down past, current, and prospective clients, but don't stop there. List anyone and everyone on whom you rely to support, refer, and promote you and your business. Your list can include potential partners, noncompeting professionals (others who play in your space, but in a different capacity), suppliers, vendors, consultants, well-networked friends, and so on. And don't forget the news media—the super-audience—as they are a conduit that can amplify and endorse your message to many other audiences.

When you have created a truly comprehensive list of the various publics that you need to reach, ask yourself the questions: "What do they read? What do they watch? Where do they congregate, recreate, dine, connect, collect, and discuss?" Find ways to be where they are, when they are there. And it doesn't have to be your physical presence. Are they finding your blogs? (yes, you need to be blogging); are they receiving your e-zines? Are they reading the articles that you've made available or submitted for others to publish?

One of the best ways to be seen by important, category-specific prospects is to submit articles highlighting your expertise to the physical and virtual publications that serve their industry. Every professional organization has a newsletter, magazine, or e-zine that reaches their members. From financial planners, franchisees, and home-based businesses to parents of multiples and rocket enthusiasts—they all have industry publications, both physical and virtual. The reality is that all too often, someone in the administrative office has been saddled with the responsibility of cranking out the publication monthly or quarterly. Most of them are hungry for content. Ask for their submission criteria, and write an article that speaks to them directly.

As is true in publicity work with the mainstream media, it holds true with niche publications as well—the quid pro quo is: "content for credit." So along with permission to reprint your article you should present the requirement to include your italicized tagline. The tag is your mini bio that says who you are, what you do, and where to find you. For example, here's what appears at the end of my articles:

> *David Avrin is known internationally as the Visibility Coach. A noted speaker, author, branding consultant and executive coach, David shows professionals and organizations how to stand apart and raise their profile in a competitive marketplace. Visit him online at www.visibilitycoach.com.*

You are welcome (and encouraged) to publish any of my articles, provided you include my tag. It's a fair exchange. You get free content; I get exposure to your audience.

Don't simply ask for the credit; insist upon it. Trust me—this won't shock the sensibilities of the editor of these publications and online resources. After all, they're getting free content. A good number of the business inquiries that I receive are from people who read an article I wrote, saw their own professional challenge in my words, and contacted me for assistance. It's akin to putting flyers for a pet-sitting business on the windshields of cars at PetSmart. Go to the source and provide expertise directly to your target prospects. Be seen. Be very seen.

You don't have to ride around on a Segway scooter at a conference to get noticed, but if you tend to blend into the crowd in your target market, you'd better do something that un-blends you.

The takeaway: Take control of your brand and find, or develop, a clever hook that makes you visible—and unforgettable—to those that need to know you. Any business that is worth having in this challenging economy has far too many prospective competitors for you to be complacent and invisible.

Visibility COACH   The Visibility Coach says: If they don't know who you are, they can't buy what you're selling. Be visible. Stand out.

Six Degrees of Business Success

When I was about eleven years old, I was cast as an extra in a movie called *The Duchess and the Dirt Water Fox*. This funny Western was shot in the Denver area and starred Goldie Hawn and George Segal. George Segal was also in a popular TV show called *Just Shoot Me* with David Spade. David Spade starred in a very funny movie called *Tommy Boy* with Brian Dennehey. Brian Dennehey played an alien in the wonderful movie *Cocoon* with Steve Guttenberg. Steve Guttenberg got his start in the classic movie *Diner* alongside actor Kevin Bacon.

Now, why is this important? Well, it isn't. Unless I am sitting around playing the game "Six Degrees of Kevin Bacon" with my friends, or actually attempting to meet, in a logistically challenging way, Kevin Bacon himself, the exercise is mere folly. But the illustration is an important one. We are indeed all connected to each other, through each other.

The rise of social media has given us new, powerful, creative, and even bizarre ways of connecting to each other.

Some mediums are dominated by 15-year-old girls who'd prefer to obsessively communicate in text fashion, forgoing the English language and avoiding any semblance of actual voice communication. (But I'll leave my exasperating conversations with my teenage daughters for another day.) Today's online vehicles have created phenomenal mechanisms to reach out and connect, not only to people you know, but to those you'd like to know (and those who need to know you!).

Beyond the pioneers such as MySpace and Facebook, web sites such as LinkedIn, Spoke, Twitter, ecademy, and others take the concept of six degrees of separation and apply it in a practical and potentially brilliant way for those of us in business. If you are someone who has historically dismissed LinkedIn and other connecting resources as simply "MySpace for business people," then you are missing the boat—and countless business opportunities. On many of these business-oriented sites, connecting with old college buddies and checking up on past girlfriends/boyfriends have moved to the back-burner in favor of facilitating introductions to potentially valuable business connections and lucrative job opportunities.

For decades, a slew of sales trainers have made a very good living teaching people how to effectively make "cold calls." Unless your business utilizes large call centers to make millions of outgoing calls, however, there is virtually no reason to make cold calls at all. Your network—which used to consist of your successful uncle, or a good friend of your dad who offered to make a few calls on your behalf—now consists of virtually anyone who you are connected to online, whether you truly know them or not.

In today's over-connected world, you can ask for and receive an introduction to almost anyone you would like to meet through numerous people you know—and many others you don't. There's something about the gentle hand-off that makes the anonymous more familiar and the potential exchange less threatening. I'm far more likely to engage in communication with someone introduced to me through someone else than with an unknown voice on the phone, or an unfamiliar e-mail address stumbled upon in a sea of spam.

We are all busy and have little time for telephone solicitors or e-mail spammers, and I have even less time to weed through the barrage of incoming communications each day to properly ascertain which bucket to throw it into. But when I receive a message from a true connection or online "friend," the walls come down—at least enough to begin the conversation. And isn't that all we are looking for? It's all about getting a foot in the door. As they say, "You can never hit a home run if you never get up to bat."

Of course, the potential to reach the people you want to meet is dependent on who you are connected to—and the people *they* are connected to. In most cases, anything beyond the second degree of separation is of no value. In other words, a friend of a friend is only a friend away. But a friend of a friend of a friend is likely a friend too far. While it is reasonable to ask for an introduction from a connection, it's almost ridiculous to ask for an introduction to someone so that they—with little or no knowledge of you—can introduce you to someone else. It just won't happen. So the real value of your network is really contingent on the quality of your direct connections.

For example: You can be linked to the naturalist who lives in a shack in the woods and makes an occasional trip to the public library to check his e-mail; and/or you can be linked to the president of a big city Chamber of Commerce with his vast network of successfully earned business relationships. The naturalist can introduce you to a hiker named Larry whom he met bathing in a creek, while the chamber president can introduce you to more than a thousand key business leaders. Same single, online connection; very different value. If you ask for and receive an online connection to these important individuals, you have a key to their vault of remarkable contacts.

And who knows—one of them might actually know Kevin Bacon.

Visibility COACH   The Visibility Coach says: Spread your net and connect.

Why Reactive Rules

How many times have you heard the adage "It's better to be proactive than reactive." So often, in fact, that the popular assertion has become the de facto rule. Who would dispute it? But the truth is that when it comes to generating positive press, the opposite is more often the case; to be successful in pitching the news media, reactive rules.

To understand this assertion, you have to understand how and why the news media make their story choice decisions. Besides the obvious requirement for a subject or story to be newsworthy and relevant to their audience, the element of timeliness is paramount in the minds of the press. Most of what you read, watch, and hear each day is what the press calls a "today" story. Not because it has to do with the NBC morning show, but because the subject or story is what is big in the news *today*. Those who are successful in pitching the press are the ones who can react quickly and jump on a hot story early.

With every pitch, members of the press ask the question: "Is this story a 'today' story, or 'evergreen'?" An example of a today story would be the public's outcry in response to a politician's use of a racial slur caught on camera that very morning. An evergreen story, on the other hand, has no deadline, such as a piece about the increasing popularity of soy food items at full-service restaurants. It's something that can be easily covered on a slow news day.

Although most behind-the-scenes public relations work involves long-planned promotional campaigns and well-crafted press materials, many of the best media hits I've achieved have come from tying my client's expertise to a current hot story. If you want to get the attention of a producer or reporter, help them keep a hot story alive by providing a resource or expert that adds something new to the current coverage.

Recently, a client of mine forwarded an explosive editorial he saw written by a college editor entitled: "Rape Only Hurts if You Fight It." Despite the fact that the young author was apparently attempting to be funny and satirical, there was nothing remotely humorous about the editorial, or its title. In fact, the editorial was so inflammatory and the reaction so explosive, that CNN picked up the story overnight, and the outrage began to spread across the country.

The story came across the desk of Mike Domitrz, a very popular college speaker and the executive director of the

Date Safe Project, an organization that promotes healthy dating through healthy dialogue. Despite his own outrage at the editorial, Mike saw an opportunity to use the story as a means to bring a difficult issue to light. So he reached out and begin an online dialogue with the article's remorseful author and forwarded to me (with permission) their ongoing communication.

Upon seeing the provocative article and the subsequent mea culpa from the author, I promptly put aside everything else I was working on and immediately began to contact major news organization across the country. Reacting swiftly to the opportunity, I made it clear to my press contacts that I not only had a client with strong opinions and credibility around this important subject, but I had access to the article's author himself, who was holed-up on campus and avoiding the press. Within an hour, I was speaking to a very interested senior producer with the *Dr. Phil* show.

Had I sent a well-crafted and long-prepared pitch for Mike about healthy dating and the importance of soliciting verbal consent before engaging in physical contact—do you think the show's producer would have called me back today? Not likely. It's not to say that the longer pitch wouldn't eventually bear fruit, but the best odds always come from quickly reacting to an opportunity and tying your pitch to today's hot stories. And even if the story didn't work out this time with this producer, a dialogue has begun and visibility has been generated.

So—what do *you* have to offer that is relevant to a today story? What is hot in the press right now that has you burning because you think they should be talking to you and tapping into your expertise? Give them a call. Shoot them a note, but be sure you have something new to add to the dialogue. Be opinionated. Be passionate. Be relevant and timely.

Visibility COACH   The Visibility Coach says: Sometimes opportunity doesn't knock, it plays "Ding-Dong-Ditch." React quickly or it'll be gone.

Might-See TV

I got a call from a client the other day who was very excited that she had gotten herself booked for an interview on Channel 8. "Channel 8?" I asked. "You mean the community access station?" Indeed it was true. What may surprise you is how I responded. "Great!" I said. "Do it!"

Many of these small public broadcasting or cable community access stations are what I like to call "Might-See TV." Because you *might* see it go by as you flip channels looking for something to watch. The greatest example of good Might-See TV was the painter, Bob Ross, on public television. No matter how many times I flipped by, I would invariably flip back to stare—mesmerized by his ability to effortlessly create "happy little trees" and "happy little bushes." He'd find a small cabin hiding behind a tree "right . . . there . . . or whatever else lives in your world," he would say.

Of course, most community access or public television station appearances fail to garner any real audience. This doesn't mean that they hold no value for the person being featured. Appearances such as these, while never the heart of a good media relations campaign, can be valuable in three distinct ways.

1. **Practice, practice, practice.** Any time you can have practice responding to and interacting with a reporter or television host is valuable. It allows you the chance to hone your message. Watch your physical habits and practice displaying passion and urgency. Nobody's watching anyway, so be comfortable and experiment. Have fun with it.

2. **New video footage.** I always remind my clients to record and videotape everything. How many times have we "rocked" on stage or on television only to find that there is no record of our . . . uh, . . . "rocking." Use TV appearances to get a great new clip for your demo video or web site.

3. **You never know who's watching!** That's it; you never know. From prospective clients or customers needing help, to meeting planners, investors, potential partners, or even Hollywood agents, you never know who's out there. So get out there.

The same advice holds true for small community newspapers or online e-zines. If someone wants to talk to you for insight or expertise, be clear about their angle, potential bias, and audience and then talk until you're green in the wallet!

Visibility COACH   The Visibility Coach says: To paraphrase a well-known maxim: There are no small promotional opportunities—just small promoters!

Change Your Voice

Did you ever see someone who was yelling at their children, but as soon as their phone rang, they were—in a micro-second—transformed into a sugary-sweet, ultra-friendly, robo-humanoid? Similarly, a guy in the office can be a loud-mouth jerk one moment, but as soon as the pretty receptionist walks by, his voice changes and he becomes a really good guy. I have only to listen to my daughter's voice to know when she wants something. "Um, Daddy? . . ."

Building and marketing our businesses is no different. We often want different things from different audiences. And because we are trying to achieve a broad spectrum of outcomes depending on who we are communicating with, our voice often needs to change depending on who we are talking to and the role they play in the success of our business.

When we speak to our prospective customers, we may focus on their pain and what our products and services can do to solve their problem—even if their problem is simply that their flat screen TV isn't big enough. When we communicate with the news media, we have to shift out of sales mode and highlight our expertise or business success. When we talk to investors, we highlight our niche, competence, clarity of vision, and substantial upside potential. With staff, it's urgency. With partners, it's synergy.

The reason that 95 percent of press releases sent to news media end up in the trash is that too many marketing/PR professionals fail to shift out of sales mode and into news mode. Most press materials are ill-conceived and thinly-veiled attempts to get the press to do their advertising. The head-lines read: "Captain Snackers Launches Zesty New Corn

Chip!" And then, just below, it reads: FOR IMMEDIATE
RELEASE.

Are you kidding me? "Yeah, let's hold the front page for
that one, Sparky!"

And lest you think this is an extreme example of reporter
abuse, I must tell you that it is, unfortunately, the rule more
than the exception. Newsrooms are assaulted thousands of
times a day by marketing and PR representatives seeking the
mythical "free advertising." Reporters and editors aren't stu-
pid. On the contrary, most are very smart and borderline
cynical.

If you are seeking to raise your profile through the news media (often a very good strategy), you have to turn on your
news voice. Written releases must be crafted as if you were
writing a legitimate news story, with content applicable to
their market. Your verbal pitches need to be short, relevant,
and free of any overt promotional content. That is not to say
that you can't highlight your features and benefits; you can.
You just need to feature those aspects of the story that are of
interest to others who don't care about your balance sheet.
For example:

> You can say: "We are the first to offer biodegradable shop-
> ping bags made of 100 percent recycled materials that have
> zero impact on the environment."
>
> You can't say: "We're having a sale on our Greeny Bags this
> week only, and for the first 100 people that buy one we are
> also throwing in a granola flip-flop."
>
> You can say: "We have developed a proprietary technology
> that allows us to cook a large pizza in less than 60 seconds."

You can't say: "We have the freshest ingredients and consistently beat Joe's Pizza Palace in taste-tests."

I've seen very well-crafted releases torpedoed by one small sentence that belonged more in a commercial than a news report. The risk and likelihood is that the entire pitch will be thrown out—the good along with the bad. Why? Because it is insulting to journalists to treat them as if they were your marketing department. It is no wonder that PR people have a less than stellar reputation among the press.

Even among disparate consumer groups, the voice must change as well. The tone, the volume, the vernacular, and the mediums themselves much be tweaked according to the audience. Selling to college students is very different from selling to desperate housewives, just as marketing to car enthusiasts is vastly different from marketing funeral services.

The real challenge comes when you are selling the same product to different markets. For example: An automaker will promote a model's safety and reliability to the soccer mom but will highlight the style, available colors, and speed of the same car to the younger, single buyers. Appliances might be presented as "powerful and versatile" to men or "stylish" and "easy-to-use" for women.

Even if your end-user is fairly consistent and in a single category, the buyers are often diverse. The spa industry is a great example of this. While the primary users are women, the buyers are often the men in their lives.

Watch television commercials for NutriSystem® weight loss. The ads that air during the day are aimed at women and feature a pleasant-sounding female voice and female celebrities extolling the virtues of the weight-loss program. The same company, selling the same program, runs ads on the weekends that feature a male voice, hard-driving music, and former athletes as spokespeople. Smart.

So what about you? Are you selling your product with one ad, one voice, and one key message? Or are you savvy and nimble enough to change your voice to ensure that all your prospects hear what you have to say the way you want them to?

Visibility COACH   The Visibility Coach says: The "general public" no longer exists. You have many different audiences. Be sure that you are using the right voice with each.

I Saw the Sign

Do you take the same route to work each day? Or, if you've lived in your home for a while, have you come to realize that there are some things along the way to and from your home that you no longer notice? When I'm picking up my kids from school, I often "wake up" to find that I am just a few blocks from home and I don't even remember how I got there. Most of us have a tendency to go on autopilot and stop noticing our surroundings after a while, especially if the environment is too familiar. It's only human nature.

But if you're in a business with a physical location, the zoned-out prospective customer is a lost opportunity every time they drive by and fail to notice or stop-in for a look-see. The unenlightened will simply dismiss this notion and assert that they have a high-visibility location where everyone can see them. "Can" is the operative word, but the question has to be asked: "*Do* they see you?"

In business, often the loudest voice (biggest advertising spender) is the one that garners most of the attention. But when it comes to physical location, how do you raise the volume to capture eye-share?

There are a variety of legitimate, short-term tactics that are quite effective in getting prospects to turn their head and notice. The "Hello! Look at me" approach can pay off big-time when your competition is being complacent. Sometimes a head-turn is all you need to remind your customers that you are there.

I worked with a 25-year-old small chain of Mexican restaurants after they had suffered a downturn in business and were operating under bankruptcy protection. Armed with a legitimate plan to reemerge, they set out to show customers that they were still in business and remind them of what they used to like about the restaurants. Part of the challenge was that while they had a decent reputation, they had very few disposable dollars for mass marketing and couldn't keep up with the new restaurant chains. As their locations had, by and large, been in the same spots for decades, people got too used to seeing them as they drove by—and stopped "seeing them."

Our (short-term) solution: We had 20-foot-long banners printed that said simply "GREAT MEXICAN FOOD" in bright red vinyl letters. Then, staff members working in shifts during the lunch and dinner hours held both ends of the banner on the sidewalk outside the restaurants while waving at passing cars. That was it. That was the big plan. The result: Their revenues rose 26 percent during the "banner weeks" and remained up more than 15 percent in the weeks that followed. Many customers commented that it had been years since they had been in, and they had simply forgotten how good the food was.

Sometimes it takes a new coat of paint in a different color; a big, tethered balloon; a new awning; a teen in a big bunny suit; or a sign that says: Great New Menu, New Spring Fashions!, or Hey! Remember Us?

Kellogg's had a great campaign a few years back for their Corn Flakes cereal. Arguably their longest lasting and earliest market entry, their studies showed that people really liked corn flakes, though most had not bought them in years. Their message: *"Kellogg's Corn Flakes—Taste Them Again, For the First Time!"* Brilliant.

What are you doing to remind, reintroduce, and attract the attention of your customers? Are you being looked at, or looked past? I'm just asking.

Visibility COACH The Visibility Coach says: Pretend you're back in grade school and you know the answer to the question posed by your teacher. Raise your hand high in the air and say: "Oh! Oh! I know! Over here! Look at me!

Hitting the Pavement

In the early 1980s, there was a hotly-contested mayoral race in the city of Denver. In the heavily Democratic urban area, the groundbreaking contest pitted two, experienced African American candidates against one another. In one corner was the very popular and high-profile District Attorney,

Norm Early, against a little-known state legislator, Wellington Webb.

Webb was significantly behind in polls, and with only a few weeks to go he decided to employ an interesting strategy: He traded in his shined wingtip shoes for a pair of sneakers and embarked on a walking tour of the city of Denver. Every day, with the media in tow, he would walk a different neighborhood throughout the sprawling city. He would shake hands, knock on doors, visit cafés and diners, engage in conversations with passersby, and essentially touch as many people as he could.

He, of course, did many of the traditional things a candidate would do when campaigning for public office. However, most of Webb's time was spent walking the neighborhoods, shaking hands, and wearing a suit and tie, but always wearing his trademark, comfortable tennis shoes.

On election day—despite polls still favoring Norm Early— Wellington Webb was elected mayor of Denver. When asked why they voted for Webb, a significant number of constituents gave a surprising answer: "Because I met him," they remarked. That was it. Most acknowledged that they were unaware of significant policy differences between the two accomplished Democrats, but more had been physically touched by Webb.

All thing being equal (and we can never allow them to be equal), the voters gravitated toward the candidate to whom they felt connected – even if only marginally so. What was so surprising was how little it took to make that connection. Some voters shook his hand, while others just saw him walking down their street. Yet because of that brief encounter, they felt just a little more connected to Webb.

Are there several players in your space? Do you have many—or just several—competitors who claim to offer what you do? If you're in a commodity market, or even perceived as one because of the plethora of players, you can gain a tremendous advantage by doing just a little bit more than your competitors.

Here's a quick exercise: Tear a one-inch corner off a piece of notebook paper and wad it up into a tiny ball. Then put some spit on it and make it even smaller and roll it around in your fingers. (It's not gross; it's your own spit!) Pretty small and insignificant, isn't it? Now take that tiny spit ball and place it on a very clean table surface with nothing else on the table. Look how much it stands out!

Consider a tiny rock. Not much to it; but put it in your shoe and . . . Youch! In a confined space with nothing else around, even something very small is hard to ignore.

Visibility COACH The Visibility Coach says: In a flat sea of competitors, it takes very little to stand out and be noticed. Stand out. Be noticed.

Speak Up!

It is a well-known dynamic that if you were to ask a classroom full of kindergarteners: "Who in this room can sing and dance?" most every hand will shoot up. But ask the same question to a group of junior high or high school kids and most will slouch down in their chair and look away. Maybe a couple will raise their hands, and some may point at the music and drama kids. But by and large, most will keep their hands down.

What is it that caused this profound reluctance to speak up or claim talent in just six or seven years? Our social environment—and the real fear of public ridicule or committing behavioral missteps—shapes and molds us from an early age. We are conditioned to avoid criticism and judgment from our peers and the social suicide that comes from public embarrassment.

This tendency is not to be confused with the desire to stand out and be admired based on accolades derived from our accomplishments. But unless we are confident that we can shine amongst our colleagues, we are likely to shrink from the limelight—lest we subject ourselves to ridicule.

Unfortunately, this dynamic plays out in our professional lives as well. Who among us is unafraid of looking foolish among our peers? In general, unless we are a professional performer, we will rarely act childishly in public or around others. (Of course, acting childish and drawing attention to ourselves with the clear intent of embarrassing our adolescent and teenage children is entirely permissible and often rewarded by the horrified reactions we elicit from our kids.) But despite the clear social disincentives to appear different or fail to conform, too many in business fail to recognize the distinction between standing out for acceptable and positive reasons and standing out and being noticed for all the wrong reasons.

Think about those who really know how to work a room. These individuals are perhaps a little bigger than life and have a presence about them. Something about them says "success." Odds are better than even that these people are less afraid to speak out, to offer input or their opinion in a group discussion. These are the people who rise to leadership positions within organizations and can deftly steer the conversation or make others laugh at their stories. If you are one of these people, you probably know who you are. And if you are not—you know who you are as well.

Now, let's be clear: I'm not simply extolling the virtues of being extroverted, of throwing caution to the wind and saying what's on your mind. There are enough jackasses around who think that the world hangs on their every thought and word. What I *am* suggesting is that you are likely leaving opportunities on the table to become visible, known, recognized, noticed, and remembered, merely because of the fact that you failed to capitalize on an opportunity speak up and be seen.

It's stunning to me how often at the end of a presentation or keynote speech, when I hear the speaker ask for questions from the audience, none are asked. The audience is often filled with professionals trying to do business with each other, make important contacts, and effectively network, yet most keep their seats and hold their tongue. Then, ironically, they all file out into the lobby to try to make a connection and be seen.

Hello!! You just had a captive audience of hundreds, perhaps thousands. You could have stood, introduced yourself, and the name of your company, and asked a question relating to you, your business, your expertise, your market, or your prospects. Of all the people in that room, you could have been the lone individual among your peers who got to show your face and mention your name; yet you passed. Why? What are you afraid of?

If you are in a meeting with clients, customers, partners, and prospects, how can anyone get know you and your talents if you are content to sit passively and merely blend in? Speak up. Stand out. Step up and be visible!

Don't be a blowhard. Don't dominate or posture. Just speak up and contribute. If you're going to sit at the table, speak up and be an active part of the discussion. If you're going to the party, don't be a wallflower. If you're spending the time and money to attend that professional conference on the other side of the country, make a commitment that you will leave known to many.

By a show of hands, who wants to be successful in business? I better see that hand reaching for the sky!

Visibility COACH   The Visibility Coach says: The greatest enemy of success in business is anonymity. Speak up.

The Path to Visibility:
Part 3 – The Pitch

The Pitch

The Questions
The Position
The Presentation

Is Your Brand Really Promotable?

The ultimate goal of any brand-driven marketing campaign is to influence people to buy what you're selling; and at the core of any successful promotional effort is something that is either desired or needed. Quite simply, a marketing effort requires something of value to market and a critical mass of individuals likely to buy. A product or service must have unique and attractive qualities that make it reasonably promotable, and it must be targeted to those who will likely want or need it. As author Seth Godin observes in his best-selling book, *Purple Cow*: To be marketable, a product needs to be "remarkable," in that it must be "worthy of being remarked about." It is the same with expertise, services, and even individuals.

There is a clear connection between the qualities that make a product or service promotable in the marketplace and those that make an individual promotable in the workplace. The recognition of this dynamic has given rise to the concept of "personal branding." Professionals are beginning to appreciate that they must position and market themselves both as business owners and even employees to be attractive to those looking for solutions and expertise. The common factor in these transactions is that real, everyday people are making the buying decisions and their attitudes and perceptions are driving their decisions.

While not always predictable in their buying behavior, people can be quite foreseeable in their approaches to decision making. Whether it is an individual electing to go with a particular brand of laundry detergent, or a manager who decides to promote an individual to a new position, there are four specific qualities that attract people to both products and professionals.

1. **They satisfy a want or a need.** In 1943, Abraham Maslow created his famous "Hierarchy of Needs." He included need for safety, love, food, knowledge, and other things. As consumers and professionals, most of our intentional actions can be traced to the fulfillment of a *need* first, followed by a *want*. Clever marketers tap into those needs, when possible, to create the desire to purchase their products. When the need is not apparent, effective campaigns will remind us where things in our life are falling short. Perhaps we are too fat, too cold, falling behind in school, smell bad, or are not making our meals fast enough.

And just as products on store shelves need to be noticed, professionals often need to be reminded to step up and make themselves visible as well if they are to be promoted in the workplace. Employees can enhance the likelihood of promotion by highlighting their unique ability to meet their superior's need for talent, expertise, creativity, initiative, and leadership. In most organizations, the need for individuals with those enhanced qualities is profound and ongoing. Even in tough economic times, there are always opportunties for people willing to step up, work hard, solve problems, and contribute to the organization's success.

2. **They (or you) must be unique.** Very few purchasing opportunities exist in a vacuum. People aren't simply thinking to themselves: "Hmmm, should I buy brand X?" or "Should I hire candidate Y?" The reality in most cases is that multiple options exist when someone is seeking products, services, or even employees. To be the one selected, you have to be able to highlight what is unique in you, what is special, better, easier, brighter, tastier, smarter, harder working, most innovative, or best qualified. And just embodying those unique qualities is not sufficient; they must be clearly apparent and your target market must be cognizant of what you offer and what sets you apart from your competitors.

   One of the best ways to educate your audience about your unique qualities is to draw a clear comparison and contrast. Point out how other products or services have consistently fallen short. (This can be tricky in the workplace, as you don't want to disparage co-workers.) Promote the fact that you are uniquely qualified to complete a task, solve a problem, offer your product or possess the breadth of experience that trumps all others.

3. **They produce quality products and world-class services.** Whether promoting your product or yourself, you're ultimately going to have to live up to the promise. If you want to move products, or move up professionally, you not only need to be good, you need to be better than your competitors or, as Godin puts it, "remarkable." *The Emperor's New Clothes* taught us that you can boast all you want, but in the end you'd better live up to what you claim, or people will eventually figure you out.

   So identify what you are (or can be) amazing at doing, commit yourself to deliver it, and then keep getting better. There is a great saying hanging on a banner at the famed Southwestern Company; it says: "*Success is never owned—it is rented, and the rent is due every day.*" Don't fake it until you make it. Be as good as you claim, and whenever possible, be twice as good.

4. **They are highly visible.** A popular biblical passage urges people not to hide their light under a bushel. Just as failing to promote the unique qualities of a product can spell doom for sales, the same holds true for promoting your individual talents. Self-promotion is essential, though at appropriate levels for your circumstances, environment and marketplace.

   If you seek additional market opportunities, you have to realize that others seek them as well. It's not just the early bird that gets the worm, but the bird who is seen by the right people, in the right way, at the right time. The key word is being seen.

So—carefully consider your target market. What do they watch? What do they read? Where do they congregate, re-create, and dine? Be sure that you are where they are, and that you are seen the way you need to be seen—as darned good, if not amazing, at what you do.

Visibility COACH   The Visibility Coach says: before you take yourself to market, make sure you are needed, unique, world class, and then become very, very visible.

Find an Empty Bucket

Okay—here's a quick quiz. Name the company or industry that goes with the following claims and assertions:

"Our people make the difference."

"Lowest prices— guaranteed."

"We treat you right."

"Honesty, Integrity, & Trust."

"Satisfaction guaranteed."

"Quality service."

"Our employees really care."

Kind of tough, isn't it? In fact, so many business and professionals across a broad range of industries use such similar words and phrases that you could have been right in a dozen different ways. These words don't connect you to any business or industry, yet they are used so much that they hardly mean anything any more. It's like a group of teens covering their bodies with tattoos and body piercing trying to express their individuality. By doing so in the same manner, they all kind of look the same don't they?

People place messages, images, memories, and feelings into buckets in their minds. Scary things go over here. Good memories right there, that bad dinner at Kevin's house goes in the back, pushy salespeople get lumped together and annoying jingles seem to get stuck at the top.

The problem that occurs when you use common or worn out descriptors or superlatives (big, amazing, one-of-a-kind, best) is that your prospective customers will tend to lump you with others who do or say the same thing. Despite the fact that you may be better at what you do, if your competitors say that they're better (and they do), who's to know which of you is right? If you use largely the same vernacular, you look the same to your prospects and you get lumped together in customers' minds. After all, they only know what they hear and they are hearing the same things from most.

Remember, the primary purpose of your messaging and marketing efforts is to encourage an initial trial. (Reminders come later.) Once you get new customers in the door, or to try your service, it's up to you to deliver on your promise. But if you don't first capture their attention and convince them to make the initial purchase, then they'll never know whether you are better or not. The problem is that most businesses fail to take the time to craft verbiage that gets them out of the category bucket to create their own bucket.

For illustration: Cause-related organizations and even some businesses have created magazines to communicate the impact that they make in their market or with their constituents. But in doing so, literally dozens of different entities have called their flagship magazine the same thing: *Impact*. I'm sure most of them have been patting themselves on the back, confident that they have truly captured the essence of what they deliver for their audience or constituents. Yeah—you and countless others! What would it have taken to simply go online and Google *Impact* to see if the name had already been taken? Get over yourself and go find your own bucket. The *Impact* bucket is overflowing!

One of the most overused words is "unique" – so much so that unique is no longer unique at all. Powerful isn't powerful, groundbreaking is no longer groundbreaking, and "number 1" can be claimed by almost anybody—for something.

Here's an exercise: Go online and look at the web sites of your competitors, or someone that your customers might choose instead of you. Write down all the words they use to describe themselves. Now take at look at your own web site, fliers, advertisements, key messages, and so on. Then, systematically go through and cross off the words that your competitors use. Of course, if they are required, industry-specific words, they may be acceptable for use, but the point is that your customers only know what they know, or what you tell them. If your words are the same as those of your competitors, then they assume that you all are the same.

Another valuable exercise is to take your key descriptors or tag line and write them on a piece of paper without your name or product information. In isolation, do they specifically describe your business or industry, or could they apply to anyone in other categories? Honesty, integrity, trust, etc. Really? – Is that the best you can do? Do your people really make the difference? Are you breeding them and raising them on some remote "great service" island in the South Pacific? C'mon. Having great people doing great work is how you deliver on your promise, but it's only the prerequisite. Market what truly sets you apart.

Visibility COACH   The Visibility Coach says: Reject the low-hanging fruit and work to find engaging, descriptive, and powerful words that describe you—and only you.

That Was Unexpected

The opening sentence of Charles Dickens' A *Tale of Two Cities* is among the most familiar of all literary passages: *"It was the best of times, it was the worst of times."* These words ring extremely true when it comes to effective brand marketing. On one hand, we live in an amazing age where the promotional options, vehicles, and venues are more vast, diverse, and creative than at any other time in human history. But the competition for the eyes, ears, thoughts, time, attention, and wallets of business prospects is almost overwhelming.

So how do you turn that head, perk up those ears, and command the attention of consumers when so many are competing to do the same thing? One of the best tried-and-true tactics is to capitalize on the power of the unexpected.

But don't confuse a calculated, strategic, and creative event or offering with a deliberately outrageous stunt or provocative act created merely for shock value in order to attract cheap attention. That's akin to the slew of recent horror movies that scare audiences with lots of blood and gore rather than taking the time to craft a brilliant story line, clever dialogue, foreboding locals, and subtle, drawn-out action to build suspense. (Think *Silence of the Lambs* versus *Friday the 13th*.) No, I'm talking about doing something unexpected, creative, and well-conceived in your business, something that your competitors might not have thought of or had the courage to try.

Sometimes it takes something unexpected to jar a prospect's memory or catch their attention. Whether your business is new or you've been around for some time, it's important to constantly remind people that you are there and of what you do, what makes you different, and why they should buy from you. People are busy; we forget. You have to remind us.

Years ago, I worked on a groundbreaking for an expansion project at Denver's Children's Hospital. We could have taken a page out of the standard groundbreaking book, had the obligatory line-up of dignitaries holding shovels and wearing hard hats at the site. *Au contraire*, my marketing minions! We arranged for a group of hand-picked, ethnically diverse, adorably-dressed kids to wear little plastic hard hats and hold colorful little plastic shovels. We lined them up, and at the count of three they all leaned down and took a scoop from the gigantic sandbox we had specially constructed onsite for the event. Then, with cheers and squeals, they all jumped in and started playing in the sand. Great photo op! Made the front page.

A small-town jeweler wanted to draw attention to the fact that they were the only ones in town contracted to carry the new inventory of Russian diamonds. So when the first shipment arrived, they didn't simply buy a flashy, full-page ad in the town newspaper. Instead, they hired an armored car and drove down the town's main street (very slowly) with a police escort, lights flashing, and sirens blaring. With velvet ropes holding "crowds" back, they made the arrival of the diamonds akin to the arrival of Russia's crown jewels or a priceless work of art. The press coverage and awareness for the jeweler (and curiosity from prospective customers) were off the charts. A new luxury product on the shelves became an event for the masses.

It's the venerable old restaurant with a new coat of bright exterior paint. It's the Ferris wheel rising in the distance in the shopping center parking lot. It's the flashing lights and sirens alongside a fender-bender on the side of the highway. We simply *have* to look.

What's the benefit of offering something startling, un-expected, or out-of-the-norm in your business or marketing efforts? Customers perk up. They pay attention. They're curi-ous to learn more. They also tend to better remember what was said or experienced, because it is perceived by their brains as something more significant than the usual dull stimulus.

Prior to the release of the iPhone, the Internet was littered with pictures and diagrams that artists had created, envision-ing or speculating what the much-touted new phone from Apple would look like. None were even close. Some had as-sumed it would be a variation on the classic white iPod with a track wheel and other overly simplistic features. But true to its history of innovation, Apple gave the world something com-pletely unexpected and dominated the news and our conver-sations for weeks.

But it doesn't take massive budgets and vast R&D teams to deliver something worth talking about. An offsite airport parking company in St. Louis has their shuttle vans covered in bright spots. Scott Ginsberg speaks to companies about the power of approachability and always wears a peel-and-stick name tag that says: "Hello, My Name is Scott." In fact he never takes it off. The local fast-food joint sticks a teenager in a chicken outfit out on the sidewalk, waving to everyone that passes by. Do you want to draw the attention of prospective customers? Trust me, it works!

History is littered with great examples of companies that took off after doing something unexpected. In 1958, Crayola introduced a big box of 64 crayons. But the kicker was the fact that it had a built-in sharpener! Innovation! Twenty years ago, Freshen-Up gum put gooey, minty gel centers in their square gum. The "squirt gum" was a sensation. And who doesn't remember the first time they saw a car shaped like a giant hot dog driving through their town?

In this age of commodity and a marketplace filled with "me too" companies and products, stand out and be remembered by doing something that catches people off guard. Be the zag to everyone else's zig and you'll be well on your way to achieving that coveted top-of-mind position with your customers.

Visibility COACH The Visibility Coach says: If you want to be remembered by your customers or clients, give them something to remember!

Au Contraire

One proven strategy that's often employed to draw attention to your product, service, or expertise is to put forth an assertion, claim, or benefit that is contrary to public opinion or conventional wisdom. It's the customer service expert that proclaims that the *"Customer is always wrong."* It's the diet guru that emphatically explains that "fat doesn't make you fat!" It's the futurist that tells you that everything you know will be incorrect and outdated next year. It's the "motivational" speaker who says: *"Shut Up. Stop Whining and Get a Life!"*

In the early years of the cola wars, it was clear that this was a two-man race: Coke vs. Pepsi and Pepsi vs. Coke. But what of the dozens of other major national brands that had a respectable—though never dominant—market share? It was clear that other soft drinks had strong consumer appeal but would never be able to truly compete in the cola wars. The solution? Highlight the obvious and capitalize on the fact that your beverage, 7-Up, is *not* a cola. In fact, it was so not-a-cola that it was touted as "The Un-Cola."

Although market data clearly showed that only colas were true players in the big volume category, one of the most successful and recognizable campaigns ever was born from eschewing the conventional and proudly asserting that 7-Up was *not* a cola. Today, collectors proudly showcase their upside down Coca-Cola style glass with the 7-Up logo emblazoned upon it.

Highlighting not only what is different, but what is truly contrary to what we believe or have always accepted, can be a great recipe for exposure.

For much of the twentieth century, it was an accepted belief among the scientific community that climate change had been chiefly responsible for the demise of the dinosaur. Other theories existed, but no smoking gun existed. Then in the 1980s, the father and son team of Luis and Walter Alvarez suggested that a cataclysmic event—a giant meteorite, perhaps miles across—struck the Earth and was responsible for the dinosaurs' extinction. The theory and its proponents were widely ridiculed by the scientific community, and the idea did not gain much traction.

But then they found the smoking gun—a layer of iridium at the same archeological level all around the world. Iridium is rare on Earth, but abundant in meteorites. Below the geographic layer, there were lots of dinosaur bones. Above the layer—none. Ground zero was the Chicxulub Crater off the Yucatan Peninsula, created by a 10-kilometer asteroid about 65 million years ago. The cataclysmic event was so profound that it resulted in a worldwide cloud of debris that blocked out the sun for years. The discovery made headlines and resulted in almost universal acceptance of that scenario among the scientific community, and it rewrote textbooks.

No matter what industry or category is being addressed, the elements to create visibility and buzz remain: If something is different, new, contrary, surprising, provocative, and with a strong visual element, it can become newsworthy.

But don't be so enamored with the concept of the contrarian approach that you cross the line from curiosity to ridiculous. You can certainly claim that eating five sticks of butter a day will help you shed unwanted pounds, but no one will believe you. New claims can seem unexpected but not unlikely. Your declarations must be credible without being obvious.

As was fascinatingly illustrated in Malcolm Gladwell's *Blink—The Power of Thinking Without Thinking*, we all make snap judgments, give great weight to first impressions, and rarely move far from them. The more outrageous the claim, the more time and information it will take to move people off their initial inclination. And in our initial marketing messages, we rarely get the opportunity to explain anything in depth.

Being contrary can also expand well beyond the verbiage and into the visual. Back in 1994 when furniture system giant Herman Miller first introduced their Aeron office chair, it made headlines, not for its well-conceived functionality but for its surprising appearance. Despite being initially ridiculed as the ugliest office chair ever offered, prices were set upwards of $1,000 apiece. It really was quite unlike anything previously seen; it featured an industrial look and revolutionary pellicle upholstery, a high-quality mesh fabric that safely supported the user and allowed air circulation around the body. This design was contrary to anything the market had previously seen in almost every respect, from design and price to materials and even the go-to-market strategy.

As the Aeron began to pick up design awards, the press gave it widespread exposure, and the public began to warm to it. When it started showing up in high-end offices and people had the chance to sit in one, sales exploded. Although there were already a slew of high-end, comfortable office chairs to choose from, this chair lived up to all its comfort and functionality claims. The contrary approach to styling and the calculated media exposure that resulted, created widespread visibility and strong sales.

A similar event took place during the 1980s. While most major consumer brands stumbled over themselves to create the flashiest, most colorful, and creatively packaged products, the rise of the "no-frills" movement took a decidedly different tact. Strikingly plain, nondescript packaging with simple black lettering, "generics" became the rage as price-conscious consumers opted for reasonably good quality products at lower prices. "Why pay for the packaging and brand names?" the campaigns shouted. It worked, and sales were strong. It was different. It bucked the conventional wisdom that packaging must be colorful, attractive, and descriptive to effectively drive sales. Ultimately, the luster (or lack thereof) wore off as the unexpected became commonplace and color began to creep back into packaging.

But what is new now, will eventually lose its luster as well. We are no longer impressed that aluminum soda cans have a built-in pop-top, that we can get money at any time of the day or night from an ATM machine, that supermarket checkers can simple scan the price of an item, and that we can make a telephone call from our car. Innovation always continues, and our creative approaches to drawing attention must always change.

In 1899, U.S. Patent Office Commissioner Charles Duell famously proclaimed: "Everything that can be invented, has been invented." How ridiculous does such a comment seem today? Innovation sees no sign of slowing.

Every day, the best and the brightest are inventing, proving, disproving, improving, discovering, creating, building, designing, and enhancing all that we do, sell, and promote. Much of that work involves moving beyond, and even the outright rejection of long-held beliefs and assumptions. It is the highlighting of what is contrary to conventional wisdom that draws the eyes, ears, and even the wallets of our audiences.

Visibility COACH   The Visibility Coach says: If you want to capture people's attention, shake them up a bit.

Is It Nice to Hear from You?

"Hi Honey!" my wife says to me, her voice dripping with love and appreciation from halfway around the world. I've been on two flights for more than 23 hours on my way to speak to an association of financial advisors in Melbourne, Australia, and after waiting another five hours for my wife to wake up, I finally get to reach out and call her. Her voice—when she's in a good mood and misses me—is one of the sweetest sounds I know.

The fact is that there are some people we love to hear from: Our kids, for example, when their voices are very small, or when they are calling home while away at college. Hearing "our song" when it comes on the radio unexpectedly, listening to a summer rain on a hot day, or ocean waves crashing onto the shore. Those are nice sounds.

Then there are people we like to hear from. Facebook, LinkedIn, and other social networking sites have facilitated many reconnections and reunions with old friends and colleagues almost forgotten. My wife loves to receive all the new magazines and catalogs she subscribes to in our mailbox. And who wouldn't like to see the "Prize Patrol" from Publishers Clearing House walking up their driveway?

But there are also too many whose outreach to us is less than welcome. Telemarketers who call at dinner time (or any time, for that matter); the IRS or collection representatives on the phone; and with a couple of teenagers at home, the cell phone bill is a particularly unpleasant review each month.

Then there are some who are fairly close to us, but who we just don't have the energy to engage, or whose presence has become more of a challenge than a positive occurrence in our lives. These are the people, friends, family, or colleagues whose call we decide not to answer when we see their name on the caller ID and whose e-mails get backed up because there just isn't time or patience to address them or their issue.

As business owners and professionals, we need to step back and take a look at ourselves, our interactions, and efforts and ask the question: Are our clients, customers, prospects and partners glad to hear from us? Are our correspondence, coupons, sales pitches, Tweets, mailings, invoices, inquiries, invitations, coffee chats, work updates, and check-ins welcome? Are we a "get to" for our customers—or a "have to"? For our prospects, are we a welcome solution to a long-standing problem, the right resource at the right time, or are we yet another bothersome sales call?

In working with the news media, there are times when they'd love to hear a great story idea, a suggestion for an expert to talk to, or a hot tip about a big story that might be breaking soon. That time is likely not 4:30 P.M. on a weekday for a daily newspaper or local broadcast when they are on deadline. That time is not 8:30 on Saturday evening when their top talent is at home with their families or the magazine staff have all gone away for the weekend.

Aside from the importance of the message itself, timing is a big issue when it comes to determining how welcome your voice is to your clients. A customer who purchased a three-month supply of diet supplements might appreciate a reminder call or e-mail two-and-a-half months later, but would likely feel annoyed if he was hit up again just one week after the initial purchase.

There is a false perception that people don't want to be sold
to. Or, we can get into a battle over semantics if you assert
that they want to be "assisted in their buying." Fine, whatever
you want to call it. The point is that people are likely to be
very open to what you're selling if they have a problem that
you can solve and they are in an environment conducive to
listening—that is, not at the dinner table.

I guarantee you that when you're wandering the aisle of
your local supermarket and can't find an item that your spouse
sent you to pick up on your way home, you'll be very happy to
hear from a salesclerk who can help you locate the item that
you're looking for. Of course, you will not be comfortable with
that same salesclerk hovering over your left shoulder for the
next 20 minutes making additional suggestions as you walk.

Visibility COACH   The Visibility Coach says: There is
no shortage of bad sounds, annoying people, and grating voices surrounding us in our lives. Don't be one of them.

Creating Big Problems

Success for most businesses boils down to two basic challenges: demonstrating the need for your product or service,
and justifying the price you charge. Of course, there is also
the importance of keeping your costs low, hiring the right
staff, effective marketing and so on, but the core of any successful business proposition—and the likelihood of success—
is contingent first and foremost on creating a successful transaction. If you don't meet a market need (or want) and offer it

at a price that customers can afford to pay, then you won't be around for very long.

Logic dictates that in order to successfully market your product or service, you should highlight both a prospective customer's specific need and your ability to meet that need. But a challenge often arises when there is disconnect between your assertion of their need and their doubt that it actually exists—or the likelihood that something will truly become an issue for them.

For example, while it's not hard for deodorant companies to remind you that you will stink (and therefore become socially undesirable) if you forget to wear their product, and petroleum companies to point out that your car will fail to run properly without sufficient levels of motor oil, other companies have to work very hard to remind you of problems or the chances that you will face them.

Life insurance agents are always battling the perception in young adults that they will live a long, long time. Aluminum siding manufacturers remind you that you have to repaint your home every few years (and how much you hate that), and even dandruff shampoos will note, "That little itch might be telling you something."

Fear-based marketing is the mainstay for helping us avoid things in our lives that we dread, such as termites, burglars, yellow teeth, and so on. But if we don't believe in the premise, then the tactic falls short. You can tell me that I need "Fit" vegetable spray because water won't sufficiently clean my vegetables, as it has for about a million years, but I don't really believe it. Nice try, though.

A popular adage in the speaking business says that our job as professional speakers is to point out a problem, or a source of pain for the audience, rip open the wound, pour some salt on it, and then offer our words of wisdom as the solution. A bit cynical, perhaps, but essentially true. I submit that the same basic premise holds for most in business. Why would anybody buy a product if they didn't feel that they had a problem or challenge that needed solving, and that the desire for the solution outweighed the cost?

Interestingly, for some, the most effective marketing strategy is to focus not on your client's problems or needs but instead on the widespread problems and large-scale challenges of an industry or a population. I call this "focusing on the macro to sell the micro." When you can help your prospects understand the vast scope of a problem, or the big risks that they (and others in their industry) have already faced, then the need for your offerings becomes clearer and your price seems less of an issue.

For instance: A consultant offers multiple sensitivity training sessions and a comprehensive review of a company's discrimination policy for $25,000, which seems a little pricey to the corporation's HR director. But when the consultant illustrates that discrimination lawsuits cost their specific industry $13 billion last year in lost time, productivity, and paid claims; that the average successful lawsuit costs a company well over two million dollars in damages; and that an updated policy manual and proof of staff training can be a legitimate defense in legal proceedings—then the fee seems *far* more reasonable as a protective measure.

When Rolaids tells us that their active ingredient "gives millions of people 100% relief," we think, "Well, if it works for millions of people, it'll likely work for me."

Rogaine® doesn't tell you exactly what you'll get (because individual result wills vary); but they do tell us that 85 percent of men who use it properly are able to re-grow hair.

Advocates for breast cancer research and services will remind us that one in seven women will face this dreaded disease in her lifetime and virtually all of us will know someone who is directly impacted.

People have to believe in order to connect, and they need to connect before they purchase. It's my version of Johnny Cochran's famous admonition. I say: "If it doesn't apply, they will not buy!"

Visibility COACH The Visibility Coach says: Focus on the big numbers to amplify the need, maximize the problem, and minimize the resistance to your price.

Is Your Business On-Demand?

It's amazing how things have changed over the course of just one generation. No longer do we need to visit the neighborhood multiplex or even go to the video rental store. Our movies are on-demand, right on our televisions and computers. Hot food comes prepackaged and is only a drive-through or microwave oven away. Shopping is available 24 hours a day, both online and in person; everything you could ever want is readily purchased with only a credit card and a click. Trips to the public library to conduct research, so common a short few years ago, have been rendered virtually obsolete by the Internet. Phone calls, historically tethered to the wall, can take place anytime, anywhere. When was the last time you searched for change to use a pay phone?

The downside to all of this progress is that when we don't have immediate connection to our office, our loved ones, and the things we want to buy, we get frustrated. We've come to expect immediate access and anything less leaves us angry, impatient, and searching for alternatives.

In his books and presentations, *Generation Why*, expert Eric Chester speaks of how impatient the current young, emerging workforce tends to be. As a father of three members of this generation, I certainly know this to be true. But I think that most of us exhibit these impatient tendencies as well, since we too are a reflection of the new abundance and conveniences that life provides in the twenty-first century.

Your customers, clients, and prospects are no different. They want what they want, and they want it now. Good things no longer come to those who wait. That's a dial-up mentality in a high-speed world. And while I don't claim to be some brilliant prognosticator or highly-touted futurist, I am simply reminding those in business that your customers are looking for solutions, products, services, and information, and they expect immediate access to them. Consumers want all their choices, and they want the information about these choices to be on-demand. And if you don't offer it, they'll find someone else who does.

The best way for all small businesses to be on-demand is through their Web-based resources. No longer is it sufficient to merely have a Web presence. Online brochures are *so* last-century, and the tired assertion that your web site must be entertaining no longer holds true either. Contrary to what high-priced Web designers want you to believe, people don't want to be entertained by mini-movie flash intros, pulsating music, and animated icons. They want to get to what they came for—immediately.

This may be painful to hear, but even though you spent thousands of dollars on your flashy intro that greets online visitors before they get to your home page, it's time to throw it away. Nobody is watching it anyway. Intros are always skipped, and uninvited music merely assaults your customers. The same holds true for your ultra-creative, edgy home page with its fast-paced, but confusing graphics and one-of-a-kind menu system. Dump it! It is form over function, and it's hurting your business.

Your new web site—and it's likely that you now need one—must be clean, attractive, contemporary, and astonishingly easy to navigate. In fact, most of the relevant information needs to be on the home page or one *obvious* click away. If your customers can't find what they want quickly, they're gone. Bye-bye searching through your site; hello Google.

Here are some things to consider when reevaluating your web site and online resources.

- Do your visitors know who you are, what you do, and who you do it for—in the first five seconds? (Don't make them read your long text—they won't.)

- Do you make your prospects call you or visit your location to get prices, information, or answers? (They won't.)

- Do you spend money printing and mailing brochures and other promotional materials, or is everything they need and want to know just a click away?

- If you have a promotional video, can people easily watch it on your web site or link to YouTube?

- Can those who are ready to buy, buy from you now—and I mean *right now*?

- Are you writing articles, tip sheets, white papers, market analysis, blogs? Do you have downloadable Podcasts, webinars, news media clips, and catalogs? Remember: The broad, online distribution of your expertise markets your business every hour of every day.

- Are you capturing information (e-mail addresses) from all interested prospects and online customers so that you can reach them again later?

Regardless of the nature of your business, keep the lights on, the doors open, and your messages flashing in big neon letters—online and on demand. OPEN! OPEN! OPEN!

Visibility COACH   The Visibility Coach says: While you can't personally be available 24 hours a day, your business must be.

Remember That One Time?

Think back to your childhood. In fact, think of your early years all the way back from your youngest memories through high school. Throughout that time how many presents do you think you received? Between your birthdays and the December holidays, you might have received well over a hundred gifts by the time you were 20 years old. Now here's the hard part: Name five of them.

Images of a new bike or a train set might come to mind. Maybe it was an Easy-Bake Oven® or Barbie Dream House®. Perhaps it was a Cabbage Patch Doll®, or new video game system. But can you name more than five gifts? Surprisingly, most people can't.

Now, think back to the times when you got to do something alone with one of your parents—a special time for just the two of you. Maybe you made cookies with your Mom or helped your Dad repair something in the garage. Did she let you lick the brownie batter off the electric mixer beaters, and you had to struggle to get your tongue inside the odd shape of the beaters to reach the chocolate? Can you smell the brownies baking, or hear the sound of the engine you "helped" to repair? Did you ever have a really special camping trip or family vacation? Do you remember receiving Monopoly®, Trivial Pursuit®, or Candy Land® games? Can you remember playing it with your brothers or sisters at the kitchen table on a rainy day?

"Hey, remember the time when we . . . ." "Oh, I still laugh when I think about how you used to . . . ." "Well, YOU used to eat all the . . . ."

Some of the strongest memories aren't even positive ones. Do you remember the time you broke your arm and had to keep the cast on all summer? Can you still feel the hurt you felt when a favorite pet died? Wasn't it just yesterday when you had to say goodbye to a best friend or someone you loved who moved away?

The point is that "things" have little real meaning in our lives and are rarely remembered for very long. Experiences, on the other hand, can have a profound impact on our memories, perceptions, and behaviors. I'm not offering a commentary on our materialistic culture, or waxing philo-sophical about the importance of quality time with our kids. This is simply a reminder of what we intrinsically know: Most mere items are not truly valued. Experiences, by contrast, are felt, given meaning, and ultimately remembered.

A minor league baseball team promotes "My first ballgame with Dad" night. Then they have staffers go through the stands with a Polaroid camera and commemorative folders for the picture of Daddy and his little "Champ." Day spas are a perfect way to create pampering and connecting time for mothers and their daughters. Almost all travel-related compa-nies recognize the value of emphasizing the memories that are created on vacation. Ethnic restaurants try to create the at-mosphere of their country or culture. The Ritz Carlton Hotels want you to immerse yourself in luxury, Disneyland works hard to live up to the tagline of the "Happiest Place on Earth," and there are very few who can walk off a Singapore Airlines flight without remembering the attention, connec-tion, and pampering.

So what are you doing to create a meaningful *experience* for your clients and prospects? Not that you're likely to elevate your business proposition to the level of Mom and Dad in terms of significance in our lives, but that doesn't mean that you lack opportunities to create momentary experiences and meaningful memories for your customers.

Visibility COACH   The Visibility Coach says: Don't just sell your wares. Give your customers an experience to remem-ber, and they'll remember – you!

Sesame Street Strategy

The entertainment industry is littered with former young stars whose market grew up without them. Icons like Donny Osmond have recalled painful declines following the popularity of the *Donny & Marie Show* and the Osmonds' heyday in the 1970s. Afterwards, he couldn't get a job. His market had grown up and seemingly didn't want him anymore. They saw him as the wholesome "little bit Rock and Roll" half of America's brother-and-sister team, and couldn't picture or accept him outside of that role.

The "whatever happened to so and so" syndrome speaks to the challenge that so many face in making the transition to adulthood in the entertainment industry. In business, however, a strong case can be made for *not* growing up—or even branching out.

Maxim magazine had one of the most successful launches of a new consumer periodical in publishing history. Targeting young men between 18 and 35, the publication offered a mix of sexy women/girls, juvenile humor, popular culture, cars, and technology/gadgets. Whether you approve of the content or not, it's hard to argue with the strategy. This is what young men talk about, and they bought the magazine in droves. Years later came the inevitable regime change. And as with most changes in leadership, along came the perceived need to place the new regime's handprint on the magazine.

"Our market is getting older," was probably asserted in the strategy meeting. "Those college kids are now working professionals, and we need to grow and mature with our audience!" So the magazine grew up, offering content under the *Maxim* name, but attempting to cater to the early *Maxim* audience that was now in their 30s, 40s, and even 50s. A new, sophisticated look and more thoughtful content largely replaced the crude humor and irreverent tone of the earlier incarnation.

Guess what happened? Sales plummeted, and the magazine shrank in both size and circulation. They tried to grow and morph with their readers, and in doing so they abandoned their *real* audience—the one that built their brand. It wasn't those specific males that were the core audience of *Maxim*; it was (and still should have been) 18- to 35-year-old males.

In fact, if you have a self-replicating market, you can often continue to offer your products and services to each new batch of customers that comes along. I call this the *Sesame Street Strategy*. How is it that Sesame Street has stayed on the air for more than 40 years? Because every year there is a new crop of five-year-old children (gleaned from the ranks of last year's four-year-olds) hungry for learning and entertainment. Companies like Sylvan Learning Centers and FasTracKids continue to grow and thrive because kids inexplicably seem to keep being born and growing up—needing to learn stuff. Who knew?

You don't see Pampers branching out into toddler wear, teen's fashions, and ladies couture, worried that their market is outgrowing them. They serve babies and there will always be babies who need diapers. Bridal magazines and wedding gown manufacturers will always have a market. You don't see them feeling the need to "grow with their customers" and begin marketing "Mom jeans" and "sensible shoes"—do you?

Are your customers outgrowing you, or have you created products with a self-replicating market? Do you need to keep changing (and some do), or are you able to look forward to the next batch that will surely come along?

Visibility COACH   The Visibility Coach says: If you serve a market that will never go away, you can always be around.

Sew Sexy

I don't think I am breaking any new ground here when I remind you that sex sells. But beyond the overt and over-the-top marketplace offerings like Baywatch, Hooters, Victoria's Secret, and even the famed "Thunder from Down Under" male review—even subtle elements and references can pay off for marketers.

This is not meant to be an endorsement of cheap titillation and in-your-face sexuality; it merely acknowledges the effectiveness of appealing to one of the most basic instincts of *homo sapiens* in order to turn heads and capture attention.

Since almost everybody is drawn to attractive faces, bright smiles, smoky eyes, and exaggerated physical features, even advertisements for the most wholesome products feature attractive and physically fit models demonstrating those products. If an ad features an unattractive or overweight woman or a scrawny male, it is often in a comic role or as a supporting character. Not always, but predominantly.

Regardless of your industry, it's important to seek ways to turn heads in your direction and perk up the ears of your targets. Attractive people or body parts can do the trick.

For years the advertising industry has been accused of inserting subliminal messages and images in both print and broadcast advertising. Some people claim that you can see sexual images in the ice cubes of any print ad for consumer beverages. Other images are less covert, if you pay attention.

Did you ever notice that the song playing in the background of Viagra television commercials featuring an attractive middle-aged couple dancing in their living room is an instrumental version of the Marvin Gaye classic, "Let's Get it On"? Hilarious! I guess it makes sense to use sex to sell a product that sells . . . uh . . . sex.

Marketers want you to see sex, think of sex, and want sex. Because, they will argue effectively, that in a world of daily challenges, the one constant, primal, positive thing (for most of us) is sex.

The fitness industry is right up front about helping you look more attractive and sexy through being physically fit. Some clever products don't even leave it to chance that you will see the connection. "Liv Sxinney" is a health company that offers a popular array of nutritious powders, supplements, and drink mixes like "Sxinney Water" to help you detoxify your body and lose weight. You may ask yourself: "Does 'Sxinney' mean 'Skinny' or 'Sexy'"? Yes! answers company co-founder Cori Dyer with a smile.

A print ad for a state lottery caused some considerable buzz a few years back, but not for the reasons intended. The magazine ad was touting the fact that a large percentage of lottery proceeds went to support the preservation of open space and for the benefit of wildlife. To illustrate the local value, the ad showed a picture of a man's lower leg with a bunched-up sock and hiking boot on a rock with a majestic mountain in the background. Women swooned at the "calf guy" and torn-off ads were tacked up in cubicles everywhere.

We expect attractive people with a dazzling white smile to promote toothpaste or tanning products, but don't underestimate their appeal in other areas as well. And although some have very effectively used "real people" representative of their target market to demonstrate their products, be careful that you don't take too much pride in flouting conventional wisdom by doing it your way. While you may argue with the ethics behind those PhotoShopped images that grace the covers of magazines, you must recognize that they wouldn't do it if it didn't work.

And just as it is generally a bad idea to save money by having your niece who attends art school, design the logo that should last a decade or more, it is also probably a bad idea to use pictures of yourself or friends and family in your marketing materials. Fortunately, locally-based, attractive people are a dime-a-dozen. Spend a few dollars and look as good as you can to your customers by using images of people who look better than you do.

Visibility COACH   The Visibility Coach says: We are attracted to those who are attractive. If you look good, people will look. Good!

It's Been Done

In one of my keynote presentations, I tell the story of Larry Walters. Larry was the guy from the early 1980s that became famous (or infamous) for tethering a few dozen weather balloons to his lawn chair and floating above southern California for an afternoon.

Last year, I saw a local television news story about a guy who did the same thing, in largely the same way. My reaction was: "Why?" It's been done. Unless he was trying to break a record, or outdo his predecessor in terms of altitude achieved or distance flown, what was the point of trying to become famous for replicating someone else's claim to fame? With all the time and preparation he invested in this endeavor he could have just as easily accomplished a feat that could be unique to him. But alas, he is destined to be quickly forgotten. What was his name again? Oh, yeah, I never even bothered to find out.

When you hear someone say, "It's been done," you can be sure that it's not meant as a compliment. Quite to the contrary, it's likely a reference to an action, a person, or concept being dismissed as unimportant, irrelevant, and not worthy of further discussion. In business, you don't want any of those concepts associated with you, your name, or your endeavor.

Time for a short quiz: Who was the second man to walk on the moon? Not including Sir Edmund Hillary and his Sherpa, name any one of the other first hundred people that climbed Mount Everest. You can probably remember your first bicycle; but how well do you recall the second or third? In 1492, Columbus sailed the ocean blue. But who sailed it to the New World in 1493, 1494, or 1495?

While we can't all be inventors, explorers, or adventurers, the point is clear: The first is memorable. First is unique. First is forever. It can never lose that distinction, unless history is allowed to forget. Best of all, first can act as a deterrent by freezing out competitors and helping to maintain brand identity. It happens with company names that are overused; tag lines and descriptors that sound alike; interior décor that fails to stand out; and the vast majority of similar car designs whose model name escapes us as they pass by on the road.

The best celebrity impersonators in the world are, in the end, only famous for replicating the look and talent of another. I'm not referring to the unique skill of mimicry—the brilliant Frank Caliendo is one of the best ever—but more to those who make their living dressing and performing as if they were someone famous. Oddly curious. Who wants to be the "best thing next to XX" or "the poor man's YY"?

Buzz Aldrin is a memorable name as one of our early astronauts, but few can accurately peg him as the second man ever to walk on the moon. With all respect to Buzz and his significant accomplishments, Neil Armstrong is the man we remember.

I do business under the moniker and trademark, The Visibility Coach. It's my brand, and I have built a successful business under that name. Of course, I also work hard to protect my brand against those who would infringe on it. A few times each year, I discover others who are attempting to adopt my moniker as their own, or to use the term for their own benefit. In most cases, when confronted, they will acknowledge that they were unaware of another person using the term and will gladly change their verbiage. But every once in a while I will encounter resistance from someone asserting that they have the right to use those words (my trade name!) and to market themselves and their expertise as such. Not on my watch, they don't!

The whole thing seems bizarre to me. Even if they feel like they came up with the idea on their own (not knowing that it was already taken), why would they even want it anymore when they discovered that it was being used by another professional? Why would they want to go to market with my name, knowing that any effort they put forward will only result in modest success, since market confusion will undoubtedly ensue? Why put time and effort into doing something that you can never be fully known for or receive credit for?

There are well over a quarter of a million words in the English language. There are an almost infinite number of ideas to be had, questions to be asked, and possible answers to those questions. Why use the words that others are already using? In business, it's okay to emulate, be inspired by, and aligned with a category, industry, and so forth, but replicating a competitor is a waste of effort and will always result in your efforts falling short. It's permissible to place yourself well within a popular genre, but the only reasonable excuse for actually or nearly replicating the look, verbiage, taste, or approach of another in your space is laziness.

Yes, being truly original requires more work and comes with some risk. Yes, it requires a higher level of expertise and creativity. Can you be successful without being original? Yes, but it's a lot harder. There is no elevator to success—you have to take the stairs.

Most aren't willing to do the hard work it takes to ensure success. But you are. Right? That's why you are reading this book.

Visibility COACH   The Visibility Coach says: Be The Man!—or The Woman! Be an original!

Comfort Food

Everyone has a favorite food they remembering eating when they were growing up. For some, it's an ethnic dish their grandmother used to make for them. Others love to think about a special way their Mom or Dad would cook their breakfast, or bake cookies, or maybe just a way of preparing a traditional staple that was unique to your family. (Why would someone put salt on their French toast, or dunk their fries in mayonnaise?) But for all of us, our way was familiar and strangely comforting. Recalling it, or reviving the tradition for our own family, feels like home.

Some in business have likewise done very well by tapping into that thirst for what is comfortable and familiar about their products, images, and messages.

You'll see restaurant menu items labeled: Grandma's Meatloaf, or Mom's Apple Pie, and you'll rarely see a television commercial for Butterball® Turkey without it being served on a big platter with a large family gathered at a long table, cozy in their bright sweaters, oohing and ahhing. TV commercials selling hot chocolate will almost always feature images of people coming into their house after frolicking in the snow and hanging up their winter coats, before dashing over to the kitchen to be handed a cup of warm goodness. Did you ever wonder what "goodness" is? That, my friends, is goodness.

It was very interesting to see a spike in the sales of Spam luncheon meat during early 2009, at the height of the recession. And it was well documented that one of the only companies that saw their stock price rise at that time was the Campbell® Soup Company. Maybe it was the affordable price, or it might have been that during times of stress people hearken back to a simpler era and gravitate toward products and experiences that make them feel grounded. You'll hear people long for "a time when you knew your neighbors, your word meant something, and a handshake was as good as gold." Starting to get the picture?

It can be argued that many in the younger generations have never lived in a "simpler time," but most can certainly recall a time when the pressure was less, the house was warm, and family was around. Marketers tell us that "Like a good neighbor, State Farm is there," and that a restaurant is "the next best thing to home cookin'." Motel 6 reminds us that "We'll leave the light on for you," and Downy® promises to make your clothes "snuggly soft."

As people gravitate toward the familiar and comforting, many look to the toys and games of their youth. For the Gen X-ers, it's the Transformers and classic video games. For the Boomers, it's the return of the Easy-Bake Oven®, foot-propelled scooters, and Barbie®.

Contrary to conventional wisdom, in this age of electronic games, Parker Brothers® and Milton Bradley® have rere-leased or renewed marketing efforts for classic board games like Monopoly®, Clue®, Life®, and Candy Land®. I bought my kids an Etch-a-Sketch® this past holiday and they've even learned to appreciate the mind-numbing, rainy day appeal of Lite-Brite®.

The television and movie industries have gotten into the act as well. From *The Flintstones*, *Get Smart*, and *GI Joe*, to *Moonlighting*, *Knight Rider*, and virtually every superhero or comic book come-to-life, we love to see characters we know on the big or small screen.

We are seeing the rebirth of some long-standing bastions of yesteryear, with a slew of remakes of classic movies and television shows.

It's all about counting on consumers to gravitate toward what is familiar, comforting and even nostalgic. And in many cases, the strategy is very successful.

The benefit to marketers of old products is the absence of the need (and high cost/high risk) to develop or introduce a concept or brand and educate the marketplace. It's a lot easier to remind someone of how much they *used to* like something than it is to convince them to try something new.

For the rest of us, the lesson is a valuable one. How can we make our customers, clients, and prospects feel safe, warm, and taken care of? What qualities can we develop, model, foster, and promote? How can we communicate that we embody those traditional values of honesty, integrity, and honor without crossing into the dangerous territory of political or religious polarization?

Can you think of ways to recapture former customers by reminding them of how much they liked you, way back when? Is there a way to attract new ones by embodying and promoting qualities that remind them of what they like, know, and want?

Now, come to think of it, I could go for a big piece of coffee cake with cinnamon crumbles on top and a scoop of vanilla ice cream!

Visibility COACH   The Visibility Coach says: Build your business and your reputation by making people feel good. Then remind them how good it feels to do business with you.

Are You Music to Their Ears?

Dale Carnegie once said that "the greatest sound to some-one's ears is the sound of their own name." Clearly, he was referring to the sound of your name coming from someone else's mouth.

Unfortunately, we tend to get wrapped up in our own message, our own sales pitch. Why do we struggle to get out of sales mode when talking to customers, prospects, and even our friends? Easy answer: The second sweetest sound to our ears is the sound of our own voice, espousing our own virtues.

Not that this is all bad. If you are to be successful in business, you'd better be darned good at selling yourself and what you do. The challenge arises when we begin to believe that others will be so entranced by what we have to say about ourselves and our business that we don't know when to shut up. I'm speaking both literally and metaphorically, of course.

On the literal front, too many of us—myself included—have a hard time separating our business lives from our personal lives. For some, the line barely exists, and that is not likely to change. If you are involved in multi-level marketing, for example, your social network is a vital component of your present and future revenue stream. Restaurateurs spend a good deal of their waking hours on-site serving customers, while consultants tend to showcase their expertise any chance they get.

For others, "sales-mode" has served them well as they look to secure investors, synergistic partnerships, and generally keep the pipeline full. Unfortunately, others around them who are not good prospects tend to turn into collateral damage as they become unwitting victims of your nonfunctioning "off" button. To these friends and acquaintances, your passion for your business gets tiresome as you begin to appear one-dimensional and socially undesirable.

"Oh, God. Here comes Lisa," they say. "If she hits me up again to buy that damned Arbonne skin system, I'm going to scream."

"Please don't notice me. Don't notice me," you mutter to yourself, afraid that Kevin is going to make a beeline over to you and then drone on and on about how he has "opted out of the recession" and his business is booming. Of course, he also is more than willing to share his proven financial system with you and anyone else within earshot.

A problem? Only you can decide; but your personal and professional brand is largely dependent on your choices and behavior. Remember (again): People do business with the people they like, and knowing when to be off-duty affects others' perception and attraction to you. It's not just how you arrive, but how you behave when you get there.

But just as individuals sometimes don't know when to shut up, actual businesses are too often guilty of the same behavior. I'm amazed at times by the sheer glut of material, advertisements, pitches, and calls I get from certain companies. Becoming and remaining top-of-mind is one thing, but it's another to overwhelm and annoy customers and prospects to the point that you begin to bite the hand that feeds you.

Often, the rationale is sound but the application is flawed. It is wise to identify your core audience and prime customers and cater to them. You should take advantage of every opportunity to capture your customers' contact information. But the 20/80 rule is essentially true: 20 percent of your customers will probably account for 80 percent of your revenue. The problem occurs when you begin to cross the line of catering to your top customers, and begin to repel them instead.

I have voluntarily signed-up for e-zines and blogs from some colleagues and other thought leaders. I don't always have time to get to all of them, but it's nice to hear from some periodically. (Harry Beckwith's "Invisible Ink" is a can't-miss!) Others, unfortunately, have taken my agreement to be included on their list as a sign that I want to hear from them ad nauseum—sometimes every day. Hey, I've got a life, Buddy!

I'm sure there are some wonderful nuggets of wisdom that I might benefit from. Unfortunately for those sending them, I will never get that information because I have become numb to their presence in my e-mail inbox. Oh, it'll make it to my in-box all right; but I'll never read it. I've been trained to ignore most, if not all, of what they have to say. It's too much!

Search engine marketing experts will often advise that it's important to blog every day. All that text, they'll say, will help your search engine rankings; but at what cost? Isn't that strategy potentially counterproductive? Don't we want our prospects to perk up when we speak or when they hear our marketing messages? If they become tired of hearing from us, won't it likely affect their buying behaviors as well?

The danger comes when we delude ourselves by asserting that "It's clearly working and business is good, so why change anything?" Because you'll never know who you could have done business with if you don't step back and reexamine your efforts. Better yet, talk to your customers and ask for feedback on your promotional efforts. Better still, ask those who walked away why they did not buy. Be prepared to listen, and don't dismiss their comments. If they did not buy from you, find out why.

I used to be a fan of Overstock.com. They have a big selection and great prices. I've even bought items from them on several occasions. Well, I've come to regret that decision. As a result, I am inundated with e-mail sales pitches on a seemingly daily basis—the vast majority of which I ignore. The "special sales" are so frequent that I never worry about taking advantage of them. Another one will come by tomorrow or the next day. In fact, they've so trained me (and annoyed me) to only look for sales and free shipping, that I would never buy something at regular price. They're constantly singing their song, but I'm dead tired of listening to it.

How are customers and prospects hearing from you—and how often? Do you ever just say hi or thank you, or are you always selling? Are you focusing on what you want to say, or what they want to hear—when they want to hear it? Are you a resource or an annoyance? Are you merely visible or up in their face?

Only you can answer these questions, but they are important questions that too few ask themselves— or their customers.

Visibility **COACH**   The Visibility Coach says: It's okay to sing your song, just know when it's time to turn the volume down.

A Surprising Application

Beyond the simple—but not always simple to achieve—admonition to do something different, great buzz can also be generated by using an existing product, substance, or material in an unexpected or unusual way. Some of the most popular consumer products were initially developed for another application, but were later found to have appeal beyond their original intention.

Botulism, for example, is a dangerous toxin found in some food poisons. In large doses, it can cause muscle paralysis and even death. But in small doses it has been found to temporarily freeze small nerve endings and relax facial muscles, lessening the signs of wrinkles. In just a few, short years, Botox injections have become one of the most requested cosmetic procedures on the market today.

A pharmacist was working to formulate a cream to treat the udders of dairy cows to help them tolerate farm conditions, and he made a unique discovery. Workers commented on how soft the cream made their hands feel after applying it to the cows. The word spread, the lotion spread, and a phenomenon was borne. Now, that pharmacist has made a small fortune as the CEO of *Udderly Smooth Udder Cream*.

The story of 3M's Post-it! Notes was well chronicled in Tom Peter's classic book, *In Search of Excellence*. What was (and is) fascinating about the story is not merely the success of the sticky notes, it's the fact that 3M, well known for its strong adhesives, screwed-up during research and development and created an unusually weak and seemingly useless adhesive. In fact, the glue was so weak that it couldn't hold paper together permanently. Voila!

Keep in mind that the farther from the original intention and/or the more bizarre the application, the more opportunities exist to create buzz.

Mentos® sells millions of their tiny candies, not for eating, but for shooting out of two-liter Diet Coke bottles. Hospital bed races, improvised flying machine festivals, lawn chair drill teams, ski-splash events, roller-coaster weddings, and elephant paintings always draw attention and often press coverage as well. Why? Because they're different from what we expect. The inadvertent nature of the application, and the surprising success of the product, makes us smile or shake our head as we recognize that anything is possible.

One of the most recognizable advertising campaigns in history began in 1987 and featured the "California Raisins" singing the Marvin Gaye classic "I Heard It Through the Grapevine" and dancing throughout the television commercial. What was unexpected is what was actually sold. The claymation characters were so recognizable and popular that it became one of the only times in history that products based on the commercials (character figurines, t-shirts, lunch boxes, and so on) actually out-sold the products (raisins) that were being promoted! I guess you'd have to ask the actual raisin growers themselves if they consider the campaign to have been successful.

Velcro was developed in the 1960s by NASA to hold things down so they wouldn't float all over the place in outer space. Now we tie our kids' shoes in less than three seconds using the same product. Preparation H is used by actors to remove the puffiness under their eyes; Hummer cars were developed for traversing difficult terrain on the battlefield, not for navigating challenging suburban cul-de-sacs. What makes them so buzz-worthy is that they look out of place—or at least, they did at first.

Fashion has had its share of repurposed accessories as well. Hospital scrubs were a fashion statement in the 1980s, as were black rubber gaskets from vacuum cleaners worn as bracelets.

And every generation has a designer or two that tries to make the case for men's skirts. They always make the news, but rarely make sales.

Jan Erickson had a dream one night about a jacket that would help her friend who had suffered a series of strokes and was largely disabled. She went on to create a soft and lightweight jacket that was easy to slip on and off by someone with limited arm movement. Following her early success, she developed several other loose, comfortable clothing items for others who were dealing with immobility and extended illnesses. After coming to realize the vast market potential of warm, soft clothing with large head and arm openings, Velcro closures and large buttons, she formed her company, Janska®. Her clothing company has doubled its revenue every year and now offers a vast line of *"Clothing that Comforts®."* The lightweight, warm, and colorful items have become tremendously popular with those who have physical challenges, nursing mothers and, oh, the largest bubble of aging individuals the human race has ever seen. Nice market!

The "green" movement also works to secure public attention by promoting creative ways to repurpose our waste materials: Two-liter plastic bottles become park benches, banana peels become mulch, and computer components become art. Other renewable materials can make headlines, such as when corn goes from food to fuel, bamboo goes from Koala food to flooring, and hemp goes from . . . well . . . did you know they make clothing out of the stuff?

So what do you sell that can be used in a different way? Have you received letters from customers or anecdotes from friends extolling the unexpected benefits of using your product or service? Does using your fitness product or regimen improve your sex life or increase productivity at work? Have you inadvertently created something that could be better than you thought? Explore other options, uses and benefits for your products.

Visibility COACH The Visibility Coach says: Sometimes we're even smarter than we know. Find another use for your stuff and promote it!

Timing

There is a classic joke that has one guy saying to the other: "Did you know that I am the world's greatest joke-teller?"

"You are?" says the other.

"I am indeed," says the first. "In fact, I want you to ask me two questions. First, I want you to ask me, 'Is it true that you are the world's greatest joke teller?' And then I want you to ask, 'To what do you attribute your success?'"

"OK," says the other. "Is it true that you are the world's greatest joke-teller?"

"Yes I am," the first says proudly.

"To what do you . . ."

"Timing!" the other jumps in, cutting him off.

Yea, yea, I know. Old joke. But it begs an important question: Are you jumping the gun on your promotional efforts? In your zeal to tell the world about who you are and what you have to offer, are you potentially doing more harm than good by lifting the curtain before you're ready? Before you launch your marketing and PR blitz, take a moment to ensure that you are truly prepared for your coming-out party.

You see this often with small restaurants. When the paint is finally dry, the menus are printed, and the staff is trained, they open their doors and receive mixed reviews because some of the bugs still needed to be worked out. Larger chains know this very well and often schedule their Grand Opening a couple of weeks after their low-key "soft opening."

If you are eager to ask the marketplace: "What do you think of us?" you'd better be darned sure that you're prepared for the answer.

A new mall opened in a converted brewery that was in a prominent downtown location, but had been vacant for years and was falling into disrepair. The conversion was masterful, with exposed bricks and beams, reclaimed old boilers, and other rustic equipment from the old brewery used as decorative and distinctive structures throughout. It was a model of urban renewal. So eager were the developers to show off their crown jewel that they opened the mall—even though it was only 50 percent leased. With much fanfare, they essentially said to the marketplace: "Come see us! What do you think of this place?"

Shoppers merely shrugged their shoulders and said: "Hmm. Not much here." And they didn't come back. The mall closed and the building was sold to a local college as their new student center. The developers lost millions. Right product; right time, but wrong timing.

I'm not highlighting products or services that were offered before their time, but merely before they were ready. Remember, the structure has to support the vision. If you are going to promote an amazing new mall, it has to live up to the promise and be amazing, and not just from a development or architectural perspective, but from the shopper's perspective.

Don't launch and promote a web site with unfinished pages that still say "Coming Soon." Don't publicize a book signing until you *know* (not expect) that your books will be delivered and in-hand. Don't release a software product until all the bugs have been fixed!

Timing is crucial in promoting any product. In addition to being conscious of external market forces (it's best to consider promoting weight loss at the time of New Year's resolutions, lawn mowers in the spring, and so on), be sure that the internal issues are worked out, worked through, and completed.

It's been said before: you never get a second chance to make a first impression.

Visibility COACH   The Visibility Coach says: Before you draw attention to your business, be sure you are ready for the microscope.

Play Well with Others

The Internet has opened up a wellspring of creative ideas about how to craft and deliver new products to the masses. What amazes me, however, is how many are trying to do what others have done and/or are already doing very well. Why on earth would someone create another web site for selling books online when some major players have perfected the model? I guarantee you that there are dozens of entrepreneurs planning their amazing new bookselling websites right now.

Fortunes have been won and lost (far more lost) on seemingly brilliant ideas that were funded and launched online, only to die from lack of acceptance and utilization. I wonder why people keep trying to re-create the wheel. So many business problems have been solved time and again, yet people keep developing solutions that are in search of a problem.

The big problem that many in business face is how to creatively and effectively reach their targeted audiences—wisely. It's the crafts person who spends a fortune trying to figure out how to sell her baby blankets at church craft fairs, or wants to build and customize an online shopping cart or very expensive web site. The fact is, while your personal efforts are important, in many cases there are many, many others who have already been there and are doing that.

I am not suggesting that you get out of the business; I'm simply pointing out the fact that others are already reaching your target market and have already resolved the whole "communication and distribution thing."

Why spend many thousands of dollars creating your own fulfillment system when Amazon.com can do it for you? Why develop a shopping cart system when Google Checkout has a perfectly good one? While the needs of billion dollar corporations might require a proprietary system or significant customization, most small businesses can get along just fine with an off-the-shelf solution that someone else spent the time and money to develop. Go spend your time and money on building your business instead.

Often, the best strategy is to leverage the time and talents of others who have already made a significant expenditure in time and money building infrastructure, and sell your stuff through their channels! Ask yourself: Who else markets to your audience, and would they be interested in selling your products as well?

There are millions of potential synergistic partnerships that go unrecognized every year. Larger companies are well aware of the advantages of creating alliances or even purchasing companies that can help them do what they aren't doing themselves, or sell more to their current clients. But significant acquisitions aren't necessary to leverage potential relationships that will achieve greater visibility or market share.

Last year I created a pocket media guide called: *The 20 Best and Worst Questions Reporters Ask—and How You Can Answer Them to Guard Your Reputation, Raise Your Visibility and Build Your Business* (© 2009 Classified Press). The book is targeted at helping PR professionals and other company representatives better handle press encounters. I have a pretty good network, but some of my colleagues have *massive* networks. Some have e-mail lists of well over 50,000 names. Incredible! And while I aspire to build such a list, the wisest thing for me to do now is to leverage those relationships for a win/win.

So, I am happy to offer a commission to others who are willing to sell my products to their network. Of course, they get to decide the best way to approach their valuable contacts. For some, it may be a gentle endorsement or suggestion; for others, it's an overt sales pitch. Either way, I am grateful for the opportunity to shorten my sales cycle substantially by tapping into the infrastructure of others who already do a phenomenal job of reaching my audience. Are they competitors? No way. I'm not likely to approach someone to sell my competing product, but complementary products give them a chance to increase their revenue without the time and expense of creating a new product.

The same strategy is effective when it comes to promoting your business or expertise. Consider your key audiences and ask yourself the questions: "Who else sells to my market? Do I see them as a non-competitor and do they feel the same way? What media outlets have they successfully used to reach my markets?"

Perhaps it is a consumer magazine that features cool, new products. Maybe it's an issues-oriented news show that includes experts to offer perspective on the topics of the day, but amplifies them over the airwaves.

Yes, it is great to do your own podcast or e-zine; but others in your space are doing national television broadcasts and appearing in widely distributed magazines. Which should you aim for? Both, of course. Should you have a shopping cart on your web site so visitors can buy things they see? Of course; just don't re-create one. But getting your product featured on the *Today* show and also sold through the Signals catalog couldn't hurt.

It is a well known assertion that the shortest distance between two points is a straight line. But traveling between you and new customers, the message can take many forms, lines and shapes, which you can work through alone, or with others. And in the best of circumstances, you grab one and hand off to another and it all comes back. In fact, it's a square dance! Everybody grab a partner.

Visibility COACH   The Visibility Coach says: Don't reinvent the wheel—or the road. If there's already a bus heading where you're going, jump on!

Don't Tell Us Your Life Story

"And here's my Aunt Julene at the Grand Canyon. Oh, and this was little Bobby when he got his first haircut. See how curly his hair was? Oh, Oh, you're gonna love this! . . ."

Why do people always seem to think that we care about the details of their lives, or how they got where they are? Okay, that was too harsh. We do care—a little bit sometimes, depending on how much we like you and your kids, and whether you owe us money.

It's curious that so many in business feel the need to devote a portion of their web site to their personal story? It's kind of odd. Often in the "About Us" or "Our Story" tab, you tell us—in lengthy detail—where you grew up, how you got the idea for this great product, or your tumultuous background story and painful upbringing. Why is this on a web site that's trying to sell car seat covers?

More important—why have you taken valuable screen space and an entire tab talking about you and your story when you could have focused on us and our needs? Of course, you might be thinking that it doesn't have to be either/or. "I have a tab that explains our product and services already," you shoot back in defiance. That's not the point. Why distract from your business and my potential purchase with extraneous information about you? It's a distraction that diverts my attention from what I really came here to do.

I don't doubt for a moment that your story is important to you, and maybe very relevant as to why you started this business or got involved in this industry. Your rags-to-riches journey may hold the key to your entrepreneurial spirit and motivation for getting up each day; however, it doesn't make me want to buy your Greek salad. It does not matter to me. Sorry. And within the parameters of that small computer screen, anything that doesn't help get a customer in the door, on the phone, or buying something, is a poor use of valuable real estate.

Of course, there are a few notable exceptions: If you are a not-for-profit organization, your story and your mission is at the heart of your message, and understanding that message is key to engendering community and corporate support. If you are a celebrity, or well-known figure that has branched out in a new direction, or a legendary retail establishment or restaurant that has survived for generations, that may be of interest. Most importantly, if you are providing professional services and your education and experience are key to establishing credibility, then you *must* detail your background. But most often those staff bios are included in the "Meet Our Team" section.

Too often, straightforward, small business owners fail to recognize that their story is irrelevant to most of their customers. Moreover, taking a Web page tab, page in your brochure, or the back of your menu to tell us about your life can make a small business trying to look big actually seem very small.

If you're one of the noted exceptions, you can turn the page now. For the rest of you, let me offer these words: "You've done well. I'm very proud of you. I can't believe what you've accomplished—and from such humble beginnings! Bless your heart, and all the best to you as you grow."

Okay, are we good? Now, go and call your Web guy or girl. Tell them that you've decided to re-purpose that tab on your home page. Maybe you can call it "Clients Rave" and add testimonials, or "Our Blog" or "FAQ" or "Why Us?" Remember, it's not what you want to say, it's what your customers want to hear. Don't waste their time.

Visibility COACH The Visibility Coach says: Your Web page is valuable real estate. Build upon it wisely.

Get On with It!

I'm certainly not the first to observe that people have a dwindling attention span, but unlike other prognosticators and media alarmists, I don't simply attribute it to MTV-style, fast-paced video games, and other modern influences. I suggest that human beings have always wanted, sought-out, and gravitated toward whatever is faster—and today's technology is able to deliver everything faster.

History is littered with new inventions and processes designed to do what we are already doing—only faster. Typewriters could print an entire letter with just one keystroke. Cars can get us where we were going in a fraction of the previous time, and CDs and DVDs let us skip directly to the part we want. You never see people standing in front of the microwave oven thinking: "Take your time. Whoa Nelly! Don't cook too quickly."

All of this newly-satiated impatience is spilling over into marketing efforts as well. For too many years, the mark of a good (read: expensive) web site was the presence of a short, animated, flash introduction meant to entertain and educate us before the home page appeared. Often there was a rapid display of images from the business, words that pointed to the company's experience and integrity, and a glimpse into their story. It was like the pre-show before the web site.

The problem was and is that nobody—and I mean nobody—bothers to watch these previews. We all click the little button or note that says something along the lines of "click to skip intro." And we do—always. Here is another great example of confusing what you want to say with what we want to hear.

Web sites, once thought to be a pretty cool expansion of marketing efforts, are now commonplace. The expensive mini-movies and animated sequences are being dumped quickly in favor of fast-loading, easy-to-navigate home pages. Unfortunately, these web site intros no longer make you look cutting edge but rather painfully out of date. The trend—and it's a good one—has been toward downsizing and simplifying the experience.

Savvy marketers have come to recognize that a web site viewer's attention span and patience are limited. If you can't get to the point quickly—or if online viewers need to search or dig through layers to find what they want—your customers will leave you for others who can satisfy them quicker. Like television executives, web site programmers must design with the clicker in mind.

It doesn't matter how much money you spent on your web site; if it doesn't load quickly, you're in trouble. Yes, yes, I know about the cool part that is coming up; and how much thought you put into what the spinning thingy in the background represents; and how, if I just scroll down and click on the menu, I can see how that button lights up when you scroll across it and how that cool music is timed perfectly with that woman that starts talking and . . . wait . . . where is the mute button?

Good morning, friend. While you were sleeping, someone moved your cheese. Yes, I know, it was very exciting, graphically interesting, musically pleasant, and strategically targeted cheese that you spent a great deal of money on. But it's gone, Dude . . . Let 'er go.

How fast does your home page load? If it's not virtually instantaneous, fire your Web person and find one that can make it fast. Can your customers find what they are looking for on your home page, or by making just one obvious click? If not, fire your Web person and hire another one born after 1980.

C'mon. Stop procrastinating. Do it now. I don't have time for this. I haven't got all minute.

Visibility **COACH**   The Visibility Coach says: Don't make us wait, or search, or dig to find what we need. Because we won't.

Do the Twist

Back in the mid 1980s, Swiss watch maker Swatch turned the watch industry upside down by doing something decidedly low-end. Switzerland had long been known as the home of the finest timepieces in the world. Only the most affluent could afford a fine Swiss timepiece and manufacturers touted the exclusivity of their products. Then along came Swatch.

Swatch began to market plastic Swiss watches—and not just plastic, but colorful, playful, and creatively flashy plastic watches. One wouldn't necessarily say that these were gum-ball-machine crap, but they certainly were not the exquisitely crafted timepieces for which the Swiss were renowned. This overt and unexpected twist on the Swiss tradition of fine craftsmanship would, on the surface, seem doomed to failure. Why would anyone risk diluting the brand?

Why? Because the United States and the rest of the world ate it up. By breaking the rules—but in a fun and affordable way—Swatch attracted the attention of the influential teen market bent on flouting convention and striving to assert their individuality. Teens bought Swatch watches in droves.

Like the fleeting fads of yesteryear—wearing your jeans backward, Mohawk haircuts, and all the crazy things that teens do in every generation—making it possible for teens to look different and wear something their parents wouldn't ever wear was a savvy strategy for Swatch. And in one of the greatest marketing coups in retailing history, Swatch convinced us that to be truly fashionable you had to wear multiple Swatches—*at the same time*. So transparently brilliant, they should be in the retailing Hall of Fame! (Second place goes to Abercrombie & Fitch for convincing teens that they should wear four or five of their shirts at the same time to get the proper layered look.)

Pizza has been an American favorite for decades. Arguments aside as to who developed or perfected the saucy delight—and whether thick or thin crust is better—pizza is, by and large, pizza. And it's great, but it's pizza. So how would you differentiate your pizza from the pack? Little Ceasar's entered the market with their famous "Pizza, Pizza" or two for the price of one. Successful, but dependent on volume to ensure sufficient profit margins. Others tout gourmet pizza or creative pizza with a wide variety of sauces and toppings.

But Godfather's pizza really turned the industry on its head with one very effective twist. They put the toppings on first . . . and the cheese on top! Seems silly and inconsequential? Of course, but brilliant nonetheless. "Why does it matter?" you ask. Because in a vast sea of competitors, it makes you notice *them*.

"Yeah," you say. "But why would that dumb change make us want to buy Godfather's Pizza over the competition?" Oh, they've got that question answered already and it was the cornerstone of their product introduction in the late 1970s: The toppings are so plentiful on Godfather's Pizza that they need the cheese as a blanket to hold it all in! Rocket science? No. But any profound change to the basic pizza would likely change the essence of pizza. And we like pizza. We don't want it changed. Don't make it into a taco. Don't make it into a dessert. Change something small, add a twist to the expected, and you can gain the attention of prospective customers.

Dippin' Dots is the "Ice Cream of the Future." Enterprise rental cars will "pick you up." Panasonic's "Toughbook" laptop can withstand a drop from four feet. Heinz gave us the first squeezable ketchup bottle. (I guess they realized that slow pour featured in the "Anticipation" jingle and commercial was not a selling point.) And some artsy movie theaters are even expanding their concession offerings to include sushi and cocktails.

So take a cue and mix it up. Try something different, but not so different as to take you out of the realm of consideration. Don't be bizarre or creative for the sake of attention, but at the expense of being credible. Just tweak it a bit.

Visibility COACH   The Visibility Coach says: Turn some
heads and it could help you turn a profit.

Be Prepared

While the Internet can serve as a tremendous tool to help
promote your business and make it more visible, it can also
give you a competitive advantage in helping to uncover and
exhibit important information about your competitors, customers, or prospects. The good news for you is that very few
of your competitors will take the time to conduct very simple
research to better prepare themselves to compete for clients,
partners, funding, and resources.

Though you likely have a good sense of your prospects' basic needs as they pertain to your products, are you taking the
time to really learn what your prospective customers are doing, building, planning, launching, and marketing? Do you
know where they travel, who they meet with and are being
pitched by? What are their priorities, concerns, needs, and
wants? Most of us are clear on what *we* do, but how much do
we know about our customers? If you think this is unimportant, then you're missing a big opportunity to connect
with clients and prospects, and I know you won't make the
mistake of dismissing the importance of truly connecting with
your customers.

How you arrive at a sales call, introductory breakfast, or
any first-time meeting with a client or prospect plays an enor-
mous role in whether the conversation progresses to the next
step or to a second meeting. Research and preparation can

create a seemingly coincidental perfect fit from the outset. Don't pass it up.

In his groundbreaking book *Never Eat Alone*, Keith Ferazzi illustrates a brilliant strategy for getting close to key individuals. Prior to traveling to any conference, he looks at the roster of registered attendees and picks three or four key individuals whom he does not know, but would like to connect with. He then creates a one-page dossier filled with important facts and background information on that person. After boning-up on their history, he finds a way to coincidentally sit next to them at conference meals, end up in their group in a seminar, or bump into them in the hall. What he already knows about them creates the entrée he needs to engage in meaningful conversation, make desired connections and build authentic relationships.

Marketing guru and author Sam Richter speaks to audiences around the world about how to conduct online research in order to be the smartest and best-prepared person in the room and become the odds-on favorite to be the last one standing in any business pitch. His remarkable book, *Take the Cold Out of Cold-Calling—How to Know More Than You Ever Thought You Could, or Should About Your Prospects, Clients and Competition*, © 2009 SBR Worldwide, should be a required add-on to any sales program, training seminar, or system being offered today.

The point is that you can make a phenomenal first impression by not only being well-prepared for a client interaction, but being better prepared than anyone expects, and certainly better prepared than others vying for the same business. What do you think being astonishingly well-prepared does for your image, your reputation, and your brand? What do you think that does to other people's level of trust that you will be able to deliver on your promise?

Remember the most dangerous four words in business: "All things being equal." So don't let anything be equal. Do more. Know more than they think you do, so that the solution you present is astonishingly well-aligned with their needs. They'll think that you are a perfect fit and will wonder, "Where have you been all my life?"

Visibility COACH   The Visibility Coach says: Be astonishingly well-prepared and make it hard *not* to hire you.

AFTERWORD – THE SURPRISING POWER OF INVISIBILITY

T hroughout this book, I've reminded you of the dangers of anonymity and shared creative insights and strategies on how to raise your visibility in a competitive marketplace. Now, following my own strategy of offering insights often contrary to conventional wisdom, I'd like you to consider for a moment the power of *Invisibility*.

Please consider the following story.

It was Homecoming in the fall of 1982. I had graduated from high school the previous spring and just begun my freshman year of college. My girlfriend was still in high school in Denver, and I drove the 60 miles, as I did every weekend— this time to take her to the Homecoming dance. (Yeah, like I was going to let anyone else take her!)

Before the dance we went to a very nice restaurant, were greeted by the hostess, and escorted to our table. I was on a tight college budget but knew that occasions such as this were no time to skimp. The meal was terrific, and when it was over I asked our waiter for the check. He just smiled and stated that I was not to worry, that it had been taken care of.

"Excuse me?" I inquired, not quite sure what he meant. Our waiter told us that someone else in the restaurant, who wished to remain anonymous, just wanted to help make our night memorable. I was very confused, and when we pressed him for more information he told us that someone in the restaurant had seen our tell-tale corsage and boutonnière and fondly remembered his own Homecoming dance experience. He just wanted to do something nice for us—anonymously.

We were stunned and made our way to my car, not completely comprehending what had just happened. As we drove to the dance, I started getting a euphoric feeling. What a great thing to do! That was awesome!!

It made that evening very memorable for both of us as we told the story to our jealous friends. I made a mental note that I would do the same thing for someone else someday. Well, needless to say, time marched on, but I never forgot that wonderful and generous gesture made toward an awkward teenage boy and his lovely young dinner-date.

Flash forward 25 years. I was eating out with two of my three kids and noticed a young teenage couple—he with a boutonnière and a collar too big for his skinny neck, and she with her hair pulled up in curls and wearing a wrist corsage—at the far end of the restaurant. A flood of memories filled my head and a smile flashed across my face. I motioned for our waiter to come over, pointed out the young couple, and asked him to bring me their check at the conclusion of their meal.

Puzzled, he asked if I knew them and I admitted that I did not, but explained that someone had done this for me nearly 25 years ago and I wanted to pay it forward. He smiled broadly as I instructed him to tell them, verbatim: "Someone in the restaurant asked to remain anonymous, but just wanted to make this night special for you."

After delivering the message, the excited young waiter went about his business for a few minutes and slyly came over to our table and said: "I've got to tell you what happened! The girl started crying . . . and the boy just kept saying: 'Thank you, thank you, thank you!' "

Wonderful!

As they made their way to the Homecoming dance, they paused one last time and scoured the restaurant looking for whoever might have done such a thing. My children were jumping out of their skin, but followed instructions to stay calm as we kept our eyes glued on each other and feigned conversation. It was a remarkable night that my son and daughter still talk about.

So here we are. And whatever time of year it is for you as you read this book, sometime in the next few months, millions of young people—as they begin the often awkward journey to adulthood—will couple-up and head out to their high school Homecoming dance, Valentine's dance, or Prom. Here is what I am asking of you.

Join me as I informally launch the Homecoming Project. It's very simple. Sometime, if you are out to dinner and see a young teenage couple dressed up and probably on their way to a school dance, ask the waitress or waiter to bring you their check. I know times are tough, but if you are financially able, pay their bill—*anonymously*.

Imagine how such a simple gesture could create a wonderful memory for young people. Imagine how many people they might touch in the years to come. Now, think of how that number can grow if you mention this to some close friends.

Of course, you can also apply this lesson and the power of *Invisibility* to any couple dining out and celebrating their love for each other—maybe brave members of our armed forces and their families, or an elderly man or woman eating out alone. There are, of course, countless ideas of how we can give back—this is just mine. It started nearly 30 years ago, and I'd like to pass it on.

This book is an unapologetic homage to the power of using creative promotion to attract customers, build your business, and support your families, but I would be remiss if I didn't acknowledge that there is also a time to step back, give back, and let others shine.

If you have the privilege of offering this gesture to some young people, or others, will you please share the details with me? It helps to fill my tank and may fill up a future book. Write to me at david@visibilitycoach.com.

Visibility COACH   The Visibility Coach says: Do well in your work. Do good in your life.

INDEX

ABOUT THE AUTHOR

Marketing and branding speaker, author, and executive coach David Avrin is known internationally as The Visibility Coach. With more than two decades on the front lines of organizational communication and business and professional promotion, David shows business owners, entrepreneurs, and professionals how to build their business by crafting and promoting a truly unique, memorable, and marketable brand. With his high-content, informative, and always entertaining presentations, David Avrin gives audiences a fresh and compelling perspective on what it takes to stand out and stand apart from their competition.

Having presented to audiences across North America and as far away as Singapore, Bangkok, Melbourne, Antwerp, and London, David has developed a legion of fans around the world for his creative and actionable marketing strategies. In addition to profound insights on brand messaging, David has successfully pitched stories to the *Today* show, *Good Morning America*, CNN, Fox News, MSNBC, ABC, CBS, and NBC news and to such publications as *Entrepreneur* magazine, *Fast Company*, *Sports Illustrated*, *Franchise Times*, the *New York Times*, the *Wall Street Journal*, and many other media outlets.

In addition to his speaking and writing, David Avrin's most fulfilling professional work comes from leading CEO roundtable groups for Vistage International, the world's premier chief executive organization (www.vistage.com).

David lives happily with his beautiful wife and three very visible, strikingly talented, and overly involved children in the Denver suburb of Castle Rock, Colorado. You can contact David Avrin at: david@visibilitycoach.com.

Interested in having David Avrin speak to your group or organization? Visit him online at: www.visibilitycoach.com.

Also by David Avrin:

- *The 20 Best and Worst Questions Reporters Ask—and How You Can Answer Them to: Make Your Point, Guard Your Reputation and Build Your Business* (Classified Press, 2009).
- *The Gift in Every Day—Little Lessons on Living a Big Life* (Sourcebooks, 2006).